IN SEARCH OF SOLUTIONS

SIXTY WAYS TO GUIDE YOUR PROBLEM-SOLVING GROUP

David Quinlivan-Hall & Peter Renner

Pfeiffer
& COMPANY

Amsterdam • Johannesburg • Oxford
San Diego • Sydney • Toronto

This publication is designed to provide accurate and authoritative information in regard to the subject matter covered. It is sold with the understanding that the publisher is not engaged in rendering legal, accounting, or other professional service. If legal advice or other expert assistance is required, the services of a competent professional person should be sought. *From a Declaration of Principles jointly adopted by a Committee of the American Bar Association and a Committee of Publishers.*

Editor: Heidi Erika Callinan
Page Compositor: Frances D. Wirth
Cover: John Odam Design Associates

Pfeiffer & Company
8517 Production Avenue
San Diego, CA 92121-2280

ISBN: 0-89384-236-2

Trade Paper (previous ISBN 0-96904-658-8)

Printed in the United States of America.

Printing 1 2 3 4 5 6 7 8 9 10

DEDICATIONS

To my wife Margaret who encourages me to write even when I should be out there working.

David

To my brothers Gerhard and Kurt.

Peter

CONTENTS

ACKNOWLEDGMENTS

We would like to thank our colleagues for sharing their expertise so generously: Terry Burdeny, George Johnstone, Neil Kyle, Bob LeFluffy, Stephen Long, Tom McKeown, Graham Punnett, Douglas Quinlivan-Hall, Terri Werschler, and Andrew Lambert.

PREFACE

People gather in meetings for many reasons. They come together to exchange information, to discuss common concerns, and to generate solutions to problems. In this book, we will show you how to become a skilled facilitator for problem-solving meetings. We explain how you can take charge of a chaotic meeting process and turn it into a focused search for solutions.

This book contains a theoretical framework and a detailed description of specific facilitation techniques. Through their careful use, you'll be able to help your group to clarify the issues, generate ideas, make decisions, and draw up action plans and follow-up strategies.

You'll find here dozens of tips on how to create the right atmosphere for problem solving, how to build an agenda, how to make demands for work, and how to manage the group's time and energy.

The applications for these skills are numerous: use them to work with productivity improvement groups and quality circles, to lead management teams and employee involvement groups, or to chair any task force, committee, or board.

We start with an introduction (Section One), where we walk you through the problem-solving process and outline the roles key players must learn. In the main body of the book (Section Two) we describe sixty specific facilitation skills.

You have in your hands a well-stocked tool kit, with a wide range of choices for each phase of a problem-solving meeting. The tools are simple and effective. Each has its purpose and can work for you.

SECTION ONE

THE PROBLEM-SOLVING PROCESS

1

THE THREE-STAGE MODEL OF PROBLEM SOLVING

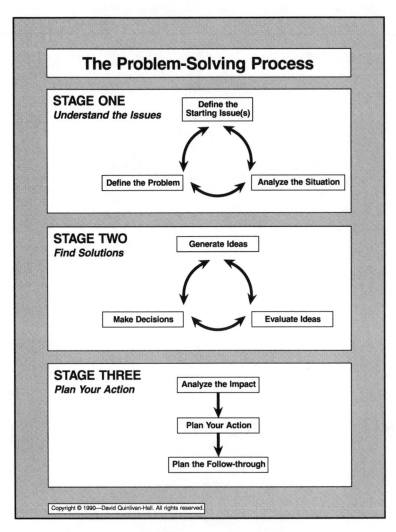

Figure 1. The Problem-Solving Process

Problem solving is part of everyday living. We are always dealing with one problem or another: from fitting a vacation into a tight budget to moving ahead at work to sharing our lives with loved ones to getting along with difficult customers.

Yet whenever groups gather to solve problems, they encounter personality clashes, time wasters, and procedural wrangling. Think back to the last meeting you attended. Recall the frustrating hours, unclear goals, confusing leadership, and the company of uncommitted participants.

The reasons for poor meetings are obvious: many of us simply don't know any better. In spite of our best intentions, we lack the training to be *constructive* participants or *facilitative* leaders.

These pages contain enough information to provide just such training. Sixty facilitation tools are arranged to follow a logical three-stage model.

- *Stage One*
  Understand the issues and define the problem.
- *Stage Two*
  Generate solution ideas and choose the best.
- *Stage Three*
  Implement the chosen solution and follow up on it.

Stage One: Understand the Issues

Objectives

1. Analyze the facts.
2. Define the problem.

The purpose of Stage One is to analyze the facts and to define the problem. Experience tells us that approximately

50 percent of problem-solving time should be spent in this stage. Therefore, if one hour has been allocated to problem solving, thirty minutes goes into problem analysis and definition. If a full day has been set aside for the meeting, half of the day is spent in Stage One. The remaining time is split between Stages Two and Three.

It's Impossible Not to Deal With a Problem

Problems always circle back on us or surface from a different perspective until they are resolved. Even by choosing to do nothing, we are acting on the situation. Sometimes this is the best solution; at other times this only makes the problem worse.

What Is a Problem?

A problem is a situation you want to change. Instead of the word *problem* in this definition, play with these substitutions and see what happens.

- Positive words: challenge, opportunity
- Negative words: concern, difficulty
- Neutral words: issue, situation, task

Positive words point forward toward a goal. Negative words cause discomfort. Neutral words do not carry an emotional impact. A person may be reluctant to admit to a *problem* but willing to recognize an *opportunity* and enjoy the *challenge* of finding new ways of doing things. The facilitator should take the cue from the participants and lead them beyond their initial defensive position.

Beware of Analysis Paralysis

Analysis takes our minds into the background of a situation. We seek facts, figures, concrete examples of what, where, when, who, and how. Balance is important. Don't shortchange analysis, but at the same time don't let yourself be stricken with "analysis paralysis." It is possible to become so caught up in gathering information that solving the problem becomes secondary.

Watch the Problem Change

The starting issue and the eventual problem definition are often entirely different. As data are gathered, it is not uncommon for the issue to change—sometimes dramatically so. Starting issues are like symptoms of a disease; to treat the symptom brings momentary relief, but sooner or later the underlying disease reemerges. Throughout Stage One try to uncover the central underlying issue.

Defining the "Real" Problem

A manufacturer of compact computers for use in police vehicles received complaints that the display screens were difficult to read in direct sunlight. The research department defined the problem as: "How can we develop a screen that is readable under all conditions, even direct sunlight?"

After considerable thinking and tinkering, one of them said, "Maybe we should be looking at ways to house our existing screen so that it isn't affected by the direct sun." With this new problem definition, engineers developed a new casing and customers were pleased. Without redefining the problem they might still be working on creating a new screen.

Stage Two: Find Solutions

Objectives

1. Generate ideas.
2. Evaluate ideas.
3. Choose the best possible solution.

The purpose of Stage Two is to generate ideas, evaluate them, and select the best possible solution. Finding solutions is full of playful creativity—it can be fun. It also demands hard work; each idea must be evaluated to find the best solution. A good decision sounds good analytically and feels right intuitively; a good decision rests well in both the head and the heart.

In problem solving we must learn to trust our right-brained responses. Following up on a hunch that something is wrong may lead to discovering information important in the definition of the problem. There are always facts behind such feelings, although they are not always immediately discernible.

Left Brain, Right Brain

Effective problem solving involves both sides of the brain; unfortunately most of us do not use both sides of our brains equally. By preferring one side to the other, we limit our ability to understand and resolve issues. Here are a few characteristics of left- and right-brained activities.

Left Brain

- Follows a logical pattern.
- Is objective, rather than subjective.
- Views time chronologically, minute by minute, hour by hour.

- Sees things as true or false, black or white.
- Seeks the detail, sees the trees rather than the forest.
- Houses short-term memory.
- Thinks critically, perhaps negatively, and asks "why?"

Right Brain

- Follows intuitive hunches.
- Creates patterns, without following a step-by-step process.
- Is subjective, rather than objective.
- Views time in a total sense—a lifetime, career, project.
- Sees the forest, rather than the trees.
- Thinks positively, unconstrained by preconceived ideas.
- Asks "why not?"; breaks rules.

Stage Three: Plan Your Action

Objectives

1. Determine the impact on people and systems.
2. Build an action plan.
3. Decide on follow-through.

Problem-solving models usually leave out action planning, but you should make it an integral part of your group's work. If there is no agreement on what is to be done next, then decisions are easily forgotten. No problem is solved until it is *acted upon.*

Decisions Create Impact

Implementing any decision will have a ripple effect on people and systems. Whatever is done will affect others, either positively or negatively. During impact analysis, your group will consider the obstacles and the opportunities that may arise when the changes are implemented. Thinking about the impact prior to implementation alerts the group to potential pitfalls. It can prevent an unworkable solution from getting out and creating more problems than it solves.

Follow Through!

Once obstacles and opportunities have been determined, your group can begin to plan for action. This involves deciding what needs to happen, who is going to do it, and when it will be done. Follow-through planning completes the cycle. At this stage, various questions are addressed: How is it going? What needs to be changed, fine-tuned, or deleted? What new issues have emerged that require a new round of problem solving?

Sometimes only minor adjustments are needed and these can be handled quickly. At other times, the follow-up uncovers significant new issues that result in a redefinition of the original problem. Rarely does everything work out perfectly the first time around.

2

THE ROLES IN THE PROBLEM-SOLVING PROCESS

In our model, a *neutral facilitator* is in charge of the problem-solving meeting. This person is there for the sole purpose of guiding the group through the three stages of the process. This can be difficult for the manager or boss who has always chaired meetings. "Neutrality" is the key word here.

You come to meetings with your own agenda and your own solutions in mind. As a result, your "facilitation" is biased and you'll find it difficult, if not impossible, to be neutral. Yet that is exactly what is needed to improve the inefficient ways in which most groups solve problems.

You have two alternatives.

Option One: Hire an Outside Facilitator

This person assists you in preparing the meeting and then takes over the entire meeting process. You sit down with your team and participate as a full member.

Outside help can come from a consultant, a member of the training department, or a colleague with whom you can trade facilitation duties. If you don't have the luxury of an outside facilitator to run your meetings, turn to Option Two.

Option Two: Take on a Dual Role

Under this arrangement, you assume the combined role of facilitator and boss. The regular meeting secretary or someone in the group becomes the recorder. Together you manage the process from start to finish by remaining neutral on the issues.

Being both boss and facilitator can be confusing for group members and you. It is certainly difficult, but it's not impossible. You have to learn to be sensitive to the role you occupy at various times. Use this book as your guide.

This book is slanted toward Option Two. However, with minor changes it can be equally useful to the outside facilitator described in Option One.

The Facilitator and Recorder Team

The facilitator guides and focuses the group and the recorder maintains the group memory.

The facilitator/recorder team is constantly communicating, sometimes with a quick word or glance, at other times taking a formal break to check the flow of the meeting. Lunch time and the end of the day are good times for the team to review the group process and give each other feedback.

Facilitator and recorder roles are interchangeable; each can pick up from the other. The recorder must always be thinking about facilitating because he or she may have to take over at any time. A change of roles adds variety; however, doing it more than every two hours can be disruptive to the group.

The Tasks of the Facilitator

1. Manage the process from start to finish.

   - Strive for consensus in decision making
   - Keep members on track
   - Stick to the agenda
   - Stay focused on the problem-solving process
   - Control the flow of contributions
   - Reward and motivate the group

2. Act as a resource on group process and problem solving.

   - Advise on problem-solving methods
   - Provide on-the-spot training in group-process techniques
   - Protect members from personal attack

3. Remain neutral.

   - Keep emotionally uninvolved
   - Step out of the spotlight
   - Become "invisible" when the group is facilitating itself
   - Do not give personal opinions on content issues

4. Coordinate the activities of other personnel.

   - Team up with the recorder
   - Work with those responsible for the meeting to prepare the agenda and participant list
   - Organize advance materials
   - Arrange for the room, refreshments, coffee, and materials

Your Notes

The Tasks of the Recorder

- Organize the information revealed in the meeting by maintaining the group memory
- Seek clarification from the facilitator or the group
- Record all information clearly and concisely
- Edit or change words only in consultation with the contributor
- Maintain supplies—plenty of blank newsprint plus extra pens and tape
- Work as a team with the facilitator, ready to assist and substitute in that role

The recorder's main responsibility is to maintain a group memory (see Chapter 3). Instead of quietly keeping the minutes of the meeting, the recorder keeps a public record of what is being said. The notes are written on sheets of newsprint, prominently displayed in view of the group.

A good recorder must be more than a scribe and must think like a facilitator, anticipating the next move: "If I was facilitating, what would I do next?" As the silent partner, the recorder has many opportunities to observe the process. The facilitator and group may become so embroiled in an issue that important points are missed; the observant recorder stands apart and makes mental notes. Observations are then relayed directly to the facilitator, not to the group, as it could interfere with the facilitator's game plan. The recorder only goes directly to the group on matters pertaining to the group memory, such as accuracy, formatting, and completeness.

Your Notes

The Role of the Group Members

The responsibility of the group members is to participate in the development of the process and the exploration of content. They must identify the issues, the data, and the solutions. They have to be informed of their responsibilities and given the opportunity for clarification and explanation. They may have to learn some new skills to fully benefit from the process.

The Tasks of the Group Members

- Take an active role—participate.
- Commit to the group and the process. (If a participant cannot commit the time and energy to being a full-time member, the group may either accept a part-time role or ask that person to leave.)
- Remain open to new information and ideas.
- Display patience with others and the process.
- Listen; listening shows respect for others.
- Avoid participating in "shark attacks."
- Share the responsibility for managing the process.
- Confront those interfering with the group's progress.
- Help facilitator and recorder stay in their roles.
- Complete homework and follow through on commitments.

Your Notes

Five Questions About the Roles

1. Can the facilitator and recorder be the same person?

Yes. But when the group size goes beyond six people, the group dynamics multiply and the flow of information quickens. In this case, one person will not perform satisfactorily in both roles. Pick someone from the group to help record, especially during analysis and idea generation.

2. Can the facilitator and recorder be from the work unit that is experiencing the problem?

Yes, although it will be more difficult for them to remain neutral. They may have to excuse themselves from the process roles for a brief time. For example, they might say, "May I step out of my facilitator's role for a moment? I feel strongly about this point and wish to state it for the record. Then I'll return to my neutral spot." If they find it too difficult to remain neutral, however, others should take over the process roles.

3. If a group is working well, does it need a facilitator?

No, as long as group members continue to watch the process and make adjustments when required. On the tough issues, when everyone is involved in the content, an outside facilitator can be brought in. Many untrained groups think they are managing the process well and rarely call in an external facilitator; trained groups know when they need help. A good facilitator can improve the quality and the quantity of meeting output dramatically.

4. Can a superior become a fully functioning member of a problem-solving group?

Yes, but barriers must be overcome. Some bosses feel they must remain quiet throughout the meeting, assuming that otherwise no one will say anything. If it is a newly formed group unfamiliar with problem solving, or an existing team that is not used to having the senior manager present, then it might be appropriate to wait until others have spoken first.

If either the manager or the group is not comfortable with the manager's presence, then the issue facing the group is: "What needs to happen for (manager's name) to be an equal member of the group?" This is what the group must handle—with the manager present—rather than meeting without him or her.

5. Can a facilitator confront a superior in a problem-solving meeting?

Definitely. If your boss has a tendency to take over, ask him or her to sit back for a while. Explain that your task is to ensure equal participation. Consider talking with this person prior to the meeting. If that still leaves you with the problem, arrange for an external facilitator to be at your next meeting.

3

Special Facilitator and Recorder Skills

Facilitation Styles

The Visible Facilitator

There are times when you must take charge and lead the group through steps you know are essential to success. At such times you are highly visible in the group. Newly formed groups or groups in Stage One often require more of this directive and visible facilitation. They require structure and appreciate knowing that you are in charge.

At no time should you force a group in a direction it does not want to go. Your mission is to persuade them—by explaining the process, outlining the advantages, and asking people to suspend judgment until they see how this process can work for them.

The Invisible Facilitator

As a group matures it can take more control of the process and manage itself. From then on, you won't have to intervene as often. As the facilitator, however "invisible," continue to check the group memory for accuracy and observe the dynamics between people. Always think a few moves ahead, like a chess player. Anticipate the inevitable roadblocks and be prepared to intervene on short notice.

Group Maturity and Facilitation Style

As a group matures and moves from being unfamiliar with the process to effective self-facilitation, you must shift from being highly visible and directive to being more subtle and reflective. By reflecting what you see, you can softly nudge the group toward making their own observations.

Even with a mature group, the time of day can affect facilitator styles. For example, a mature group might need direction and energy first thing in the morning or to get started just after the lunch break.

23

Get Fired

Your objective as the facilitator should be to work yourself out of a job. When the group has learned to facilitate itself, it may fire the facilitator! Take this as a sign of success.

Twenty-five Facilitator Interventions

1 *Describe Process Obstacles*

When the process is blocked, hold a mirror up to the group so members can see themselves. For example, "Are you waiting for something to happen? As the facilitator, I have to resist the temptation to show you my solution. So, it's up you. I suggest you roll up your sleeves and dig into this issue."

2 *Encourage Participation*

Establish a participative climate at the start of the meeting and maintain it throughout. For example, say to the group, "You are here, each of you, because of your experience with the issues. It is critical that you share your perspective." Or, to an individual, "Chris, you have been through a slump before. What do you see as the critical first step?"

3 *Accept Mistakes*

Even facilitators make mistakes. Occasionally groups are led down trails only to have to backtrack and pursue another direction. Be big spirited enough to accept responsibility but don't become overly apologetic because then credibility is affected.

4   Use Body Language

Much of our communication comes from body language. Moving closer to someone who is "under fire" from the group gives this person support. Moving closer to a noisy, disruptive person usually results in the person quieting down.

Use Your Body to Direct Traffic

When two people are verbally sparring, step between them, thus breaking their eye contact. Now, with their eyes on you, walk backwards toward the group memory and ask one of them to outline the problem. With the data on the flipchart paper, turn to the other person and follow the same procedure. With the fight stopped and the information out, it is time to involve the group by asking them, "What needs to happen now?"

Read the body language of group members. Quiet people often look like they want to say something; the idea is behind their eyes long before they build up the courage to speak out. People with low commitment lean back, or look bored or frustrated (vacant stares, fidgeting, disruptive behavior). Tired people fall asleep, yawn, or become jittery. These are signs that it's time for a break or to work in small groups.

Be careful not to give away your personal position on a topic by a look, nod, smile, or other nonverbal sign. Once you do, you lose your neutrality. Leave no room for doubt about your neutrality, even while chatting informally during break time.

5 *Discourage Personal Attacks*

The group needs to be *hard on issues* and *soft on people*. If someone starts being hard on another group member, step in. For example, "Hold it, Karen, you and Ted are in this problem together. Taking shots at each other won't get you closer to the issue. What's your concern with Ted's point?"

How to Resolve Conflict

Disruptions occur when two or more people cease to listen to each other or fall in love with their own problem definition or solutions. If you see members falling into this trap, help them along by using this intervention.

1. Ask each person to write his or her definition of the problem on a piece of paper. Flipchart paper is best as it can be posted for all to see.
2. Review the definitions and point out differences and similarities. Look for areas of agreements, common ground.
3. Involve the individuals, and the group, in building new definitions.

6 *Suggest a Process*

It is your job to suggest a process. This book is full of process ideas. For example, "To begin generating ideas now will have us going in six different directions. I am not sure the problem is clearly defined. I suggest each of you take five minutes and write your view of the 'real' problem. Begin with the word 'what' and end with a question mark."

7   Encourage Equal Participation

This means slowing down the talkers and bringing out the quiet ones in the group. A technique that can be fun is called "Spend A Penny."

Give everyone in the group three pennies or have them take three coins or small objects from their own pockets. The pennies are placed in front of each person, visible to all. Each time a person says something, it costs a penny. The spent coins can be thrown into the middle of the room, or clearly placed apart from the unspent ones. A person who has spent all coins must remain silent until all the others have spent theirs. Conduct a debriefing of this exercise, focusing on the need for equal participation.

8   Make a Contract

Establish a contract with the group at the beginning of the meeting; afterwards, ensure the contract is followed. If the group begins moving off track, stop the process and review the contract. This will either bring the group back onto the contracted track or open the contract to change. For example, "You initially agreed to work on generating ideas until eleven o'clock. It's now eleven fifteen and you are still going strong. Do you want to stop here or continue for a while longer?"

Contracting

A contract between the facilitator/recorder team and the group may include an understanding of

- *Roles:* facilitator, recorder, group members, chairperson, senior manager, external experts
- *Time frames:* for the present meeting and future meetings, and for staying in each stage of problem solving

- *Decision making:* how decisions are to be made, including options if time runs out and a consensus has not been reached

A contract between members of the group delineates how they wish to interact.

- What behaviors do members wish to *support?*
- What behaviors do members wish to *discourage?*

For example, groups often support openness, honesty, listening, showing respect, patience with each other, and confidentiality.

Contracts give you the base from which to challenge members who go off track. By referring to the original contract, you can spotlight the issues and lead the group to deal with them.

9 Suggest a Break

Whenever the group gets stuck or energy runs low, a break is as good as a fresh start. The refreshment break is a common choice; try these variations:

- Have a five-minute stretch break with exercises.
- Take a walk to get fresh air, exercise, and ideas.
- Move into smaller groups.
- Stop collecting information to look for the common threads.
- Stop and do something completely different, such as a five-minute story or joke-telling session.
- Watch a short motivational video.
- Bring in a guest expert.

10 Summarize for the Group

After a long break, such as lunch, overnight, or between meetings, a summary is essential. It also comes in handy when you need to take a breather to sort out what is happening. Remember: if you are confused, chances are the group is feeling it, too. Summarizing allows everyone to stop, take stock, and start afresh.

11 Listen Intensely

Facilitators must listen so hard that they break out in a sweat. A day spent facilitating is as tiring as a day spent chopping wood.

12 Involve the Group in Managing the Process

You cannot hope to have all the process answers, although you probably have a few more than most people in the room. When you run out, turn to the group for ideas. This applies especially in Stages Two and Three, when the group begins to take some control of the process. For example, ask "How do you want to evaluate these ideas?" Such a question shows trust in the group and respect for members' abilities.

13 Break Into Small Groups

Breaking into small groups can increase participation and enable a number of activities to occur simultaneously: one group might explore one side of an issue, while the other group takes the opposite position. Use small groups to generate ideas and to synthesize information. Make it clear to everyone that they are not to take a position or bring recommendations. They are to generate quantity and not distill for quality. Do not use small groups to make decisions. When consensus is required, use the full group.

14   *Recognize the Group's Effort*

Reward the group verbally at regular intervals, certainly at lunch and at the end of the day. For example, "This afternoon you have worked extremely hard. You can see the results!"

15   *Conduct a Debriefing*

A debriefing is like a snapshot; it enables everyone to look at what has happened. This activity can be useful at the end of a meeting or a day (or first thing in the morning if the group was too tired the previous evening to give it serious consideration). A debriefing is also useful in the midst of a meeting, especially when a group bogs down in personality clashes and personal agendas. The following are examples of what you might say to help members to shift focus, reflect, and learn from what has been going on.

- Let's stop the process for a few minutes and look at what's been happening here.
- What are your observations of the group process over the last ten minutes?
- How do you feel about this?
- What can be done about this situation?
- What do you want to do from now on?

*How to Debrief the Group**

After a game, the coach and team view videotapes and discuss how it went—looking for ways to understand and improve. At strategic intervals in the problem-solving process you too should take the time to analyze what

---

* Adapted from *The Instructor's Survival Kit: A Handbook for Teachers of Adults,* by Peter Renner. Vancouver, BC: Training Associates Ltd., 1983

happened. The feedback points the way to improvement. The objective is not to analyze the decisions or the problem-solving process but to help the group to learn from experience—about themselves and about how to work in groups. A debriefing might take anywhere from five to sixty minutes. You can probe on four levels.

- *Objective level*—Gather facts by asking, "What happened here?"
- *Reflective level*—Gather impressions and feelings by asking, "How do you feel about it?"
- *Interpretive level*—Determine key learnings by asking, "What did you learn from this experience?"
- *Decision-making level*—Decide what needs to be done with these learnings by asking, "What do you want to do with this information for the next time?"

16 *Search for Common Threads*

Stop the meeting and have the group search for the common threads; this helps focus on what has been accomplished. It also aids in defining the problem or selecting a solution. With the common elements clarified, focus is achieved for the next steps.

A good break activity is to ask everyone to read over the group memory, taking note of the common threads on a sheet of paper. This gets people up and moving.

17 *Present a "Straw Man"*

The "Straw Man" intervention provides a target that the group can take shots at. Between sessions, you might draft a Straw Man definition of the problem or ask a member to summarize the day's data and present it at the next session as a straw man distillation.

The important point is the straw man is a target. Encourage the group to shoot at it and not just accept it, only to discover later that something is missing or has been changed. Only by picking it apart, adding to it, and changing it, will the group develop ownership of it. Without this involvement, it will always be someone else's work.

Group members who build the straw man must not take criticism personally. It only makes it hard for others to take shots, since they don't want to offend anyone. You must be equally careful when presenting a straw man argument.

18 *"Boomerang" Questions Back*

Someone throws a question at you and instead of taking a position, you throw it back. Ask the individual, "What do you think?" or throw it to the group, asking "How do the rest of you feel about this?"

During the boomerang, you have time to think. Occasionally, members try to snag the facilitator, especially early in the life of a new group or with a new facilitator. Be alert: They are testing you. The boomerang helps you avoid or get out of traps before you get stuck.

19 *Act Stupid*

Playing at being stupid forces people to explain their points. Use this technique when you know the answer but think others might not. For example, "I may be a bit slow on this one, but would you explain the relationship between cost per mailing and average order?" Detectives and facilitators occasionally benefit from acting stupid.

20 *Focus on the Group Memory*

Sometimes just looking at the group memory helps put the issue into perspective. When the group is looking for ideas, bring it back to the data already generated. When people begin to tire, highlight the consensus points on the group memory. Draw their attention to the wall and capture their thoughts when conflict erupts. Don't allow the group memory to become just a backdrop; use it in a dynamic way.

21 *Reinforce Consensus*

Each time a group moves ahead with consensus, reinforce it. For example, "This seems like a consensus to me." Consensus must be achieved at every stage; it begins with the starting issue and moves through the entire problem-solving process. Achieving consensus at each small step shows people that it is not as difficult as they might think; this in turn helps to build more consensus.

22 *Check for Agreements*

Before pursuing a particular meeting direction, check with the full group to ensure that everyone and not just the vocal majority agrees. By obtaining visible signs of support from all members, there will be no doubt in anyone's mind—group members or the facilitator—that the group is in agreement.

23 *Maintain the Focus of the Group*

Without focus, the group loses its power. All divergence must be followed by convergence. All tangents must be brought back to the central question. All work must be directed toward closing the gap between the starting issue and success.

24 *Be Specific*

Always strive for specific information. Use questions such as

- Can you tell me more?
- What do you mean?
- Can you give an example?
- Can you be more specific?

From specific data come clearer solutions and focused action plans. When an issue is well defined, it is easy to discuss, to decide upon a plan, and to implement it.

Don't settle for general statements such as, "We have a big problem with rejects"; instead push for hard information: "Rejects are up 20 percent on the third shift." The group needs specifics to work with.

25 *Take the Group's Pulse*

Ask the group to assess where it is in the process. Do it when you want a group to look inward to see how it is operating—or not operating. Use it when you are genuinely uncertain about the direction the group has taken. If members feel positive about their direction, then they will put you straight; otherwise, they too will question the usefulness of their course.

Recorder Skills and Tools

The Tools

The Blank Wall

Posting sheets on an entire wall is better than using flip-chart stands where information is covered up as pages are flipped. Tape the paper in five or six sections eight sheets deep. By overlapping the tape as shown in Figure 2, it looks neat and professional and one sheet is easily removed without bringing the other sheets down. Posting more than eight sheets tends to pull them all down.

Paper and Tape

Use bond paper and masking tape and you won't damage even the best wall covering. Half- to three-quarter-inch masking tape is convenient and has the sticking power—although some brands have more stick than others. Begin preparing a room by placing strips of tape about two inches above where you plan to post the flipchart paper. This gives you a ready supply of tape where you need it. Keep these strips of tape supplied during slow times in the

Figure 2. How to Post Newsprint

meeting or at break times. Hang sheets high enough for all
to see but not so high as to require a stepladder for the
recorder.

Creating a Blank Wall

You won't always have the perfect setup, but a little inge-
nuity pays off. When Dave took a management team to a
remote fishing camp for a two-day planning meeting, the
location was idyllic—until they discovered the log walls in
the meeting room were unsuitable for posting paper. For-
tunately, the proprietor came by to see how the group was
getting on. Dave explained the need for a smooth wall for
the group memory. Minutes later the host returned with
two sheets of plywood and nailed them to the wall. Perfect!

Figure 3. Preparing the Group Memory

Pens

Water-based, chisel-tipped pens work best. They do not
give off odors that can give you headaches. Water-based
pens also don't bleed through the paper to leave embar-
rassing marks on the wall, and ink on your clothes will
often wash out. The chisel rather than the pointed tip
makes broad lines, easier for everyone to see. Tape a four-
color set together as illustrated; it saves fumbling time and

looks professional. One pen can be removed while the other three and all four caps stay together.

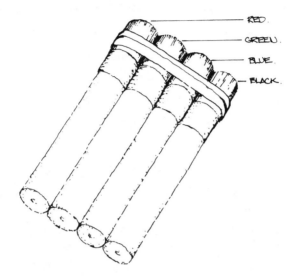

Figure 4. Preparing Your Pens

The Group Memory

By writing and posting the "minutes" on the wall, the recorder maintains an ongoing group memory. It helps to focus the group physically, as members' eyes find a natural resting spot "up front," and mentally, since the mind tends to follow the eyes.

The group memory

- Makes problem solving a visual process
- Provides a group history, leading to a sense of progress and achievement
- Enhances creativity by piggybacking new information on existing data

- Reduces one-on-one confrontation, since the seating directs the eyes to the group memory and reduces eye contact between group members
- Assists latecomers to catch up without interrupting
- Helps to organize, distill, and synthesize information collected
- Assists in the review of material, especially after breaks
- Helps members distinguish between content and process issues
- Acknowledges each contribution and person
- Neutralizes information and ideas; once displayed they become group property, freeing members from having to defend their contributions. The point becomes more important than the person who made it

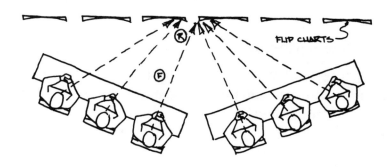

Figure 5. Group Memory Wall

Recording Techniques

The recorder must develop a few tricks to make the best use of the group memory: headlining, abbreviations, symbols, diagrams, and highlighting. Here are a few examples.

Headlining

The recorder listens to a paragraph of words and writes a single line to capture the essence. To achieve this, the key thought must be separated from supporting thoughts. Some speakers make it easy because they start with their key thought and add their supporting points later. When members speak in this manner, the recorder easily captures the key point first, then adds supporting points as they emerge. Recorder and participant finish together and the group process moves along smoothly. As members see their words in writing, they learn to present their contribution in recordable form, thus increasing productivity and satisfaction.

Abbreviations

The group and your style will help you develop a list. Here are just a few suggestions from our work with business groups. This shorthand allows the recorder to keep up with the flow of data.

mgmt	—	management
mgr	—	manager
ee	—	employee
h2	—	how to
+/–	—	plus/minus
id	—	identify
diff	—	different
w	—	with
w/o	—	without
sp	—	spelling
ie	—	that is
eg	—	for example
thru	—	through
pm	—	participative management
ei	—	employee involvement
trg	—	training

Symbols

Use them as long as their meaning is obvious, they speed up the recording function. Add your own!

Therefore	∴
Greater	>
Less	<
Equals	=
Increasing	→
Decreasing	←
Up	↑
Down	↓

Figure 6. Recorder Symbols

Diagrams

We use diagrams like the ones depicted here to reflect a mood at a given time. Words alone are sometimes insufficient to record the atmosphere in the room; pictures help

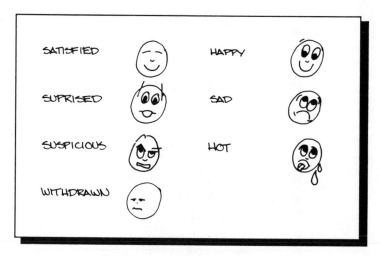

Figure 7. Recorder Diagrams

to capture the moment, lead to discussions ("Why do we appear bored?"), and frequently get a laugh and release of tension.

Highlighting

This dramatic technique, quickly sketched without great artistic requirements, helps to separate and emphasize particular moments in the group memory. The selection shown here is taken from our collection of past group memories.

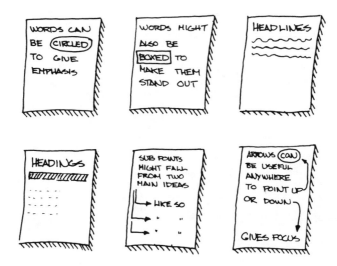

Figure 8. Recorder Highlighting Ideas

4

Arrangements Prior to the First Meeting

Carefully planned room arrangements and advance preparations are essential to group effectiveness.

Tables and Chairs

The traditional meeting arrangement is to gather around a large table. When a lot of money has been spent on a rosewood table, you might feel obliged to use it, even if it hinders the group's comfort and effectiveness. This is not a suitable arrangement for problem-solving meetings! When a group tries to problem-solve at a board table, the communication flows like this:

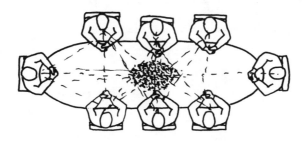

Figure 9. Conventional Furniture Setup

Where is the focus of this meeting? If there is one, it is in the middle of the table. This is the black hole of the board table; it sucks the energy from the group and gives nothing back, resulting in a loss of focus.

When people are seated across the table from each other, they tend to look at the person opposite when speaking—the easiest line of sight. When points are made, they are directed at the person across the table, even if they are intended for others in the group. The inadvertent recipient may feel "picked on" and become defensive. Such encounters, however well-intentioned, undermine the effectiveness of the group effort—all because of the physical setting. Your arrangement should look drastically different, shifting the focus from people to issues!

Figure 10. Focus on the Group Memory

Now the focus is toward the front of the room and on the group memory. This reduces interpersonal clashes and keeps the focus on the issues.

Change the Room, Not the Process

If the room does not suit the process, change it! A screwdriver in your briefcase will take most pictures and hooks off walls. Extra tables and chairs can be taken outside the room or stacked in the corner. The boardroom table can be moved away from the center of the room. Even the president's office can be adjusted to give the meeting a better chance of success—and most executives will appreciate the change if it results in a successful meeting.

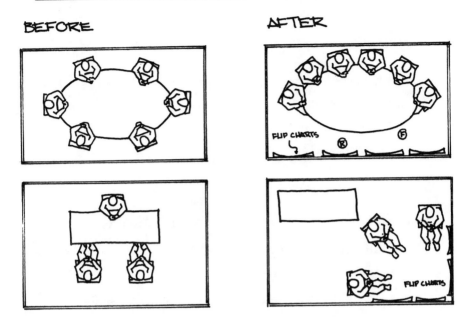

Figure 11. Before and After Room Setups

Room Setup

Checklists are easy to ignore. Don't get caught unprepared. Anticipate, imagine, and rehearse the meeting in your mind! Look at each of the questions in the Room Setup Checklist, write down your responses, and plan specific steps to deal with each item. Ideally, get a second opinion from someone who knows the group.

Room Setup Checklist

General Questions

- ❑ Is it large enough for the group?
- ❑ Is there a good wall for the group memory?
- ❑ Can you get into the room ahead of time to set up?
- ❑ Is there good ventilation and temperature control?

Lighting

❑ Does the lighting allow everyone to clearly see the group memory?

❑ If not, can extra lights or higher-wattage bulbs be arranged?

Furniture

❑ Are there enough tables and chairs? Are there spares?

❑ Will people be comfortable? (Test by sitting in each chair.)

❑ Can the group memory be read from all seats?

Supplies

❑ Are there adequate pens, paper, and masking tape? (You will need approximately 50–75 sheets of newsprint per day.)

❑ Do you have one four-color set of pens per meeting day?

❑ Do you have a spare roll of masking tape? (One will last about thirty meeting days.)

Refreshments and Meals

❑ Will hot and cold beverages be provided? Who will do this? When will the beverages arrive? Where will they be placed?

❑ Can people go out to lunch and be back within an hour?

❑ If the group eats together, can the restaurant handle the entire group at once? (Selecting from the menu at the morning break and placing the order in advance saves time!)

Other Concerns

❑

❑

❑

Agenda Building

You can greatly influence the tone of the meeting through careful preparation. Be clear in your own mind what the meeting is about and involve key players well in advance. Here is a checklist of things that demand your attention. Again, treat this job seriously. Sloppy planning will come back to haunt you; careful advance work creates peace of mind, communicates your professionalism, and avoids most traps.

Ponder each point and write down your response. Each situation generates its own considerations. Photocopy this sheet and write on it. We suggest you take this step seriously! Many benefits will accrue!

Agenda Building Checklist

❑ Is the purpose of the meeting clear? How do you know?

❑ Are the right people in attendance? Should there be additions or deletions?

❑ Will people be attending who have no interest in being there?

❏ If a decision must be made, will the decision makers be there?

❏ If an expert is needed, will this expert be present?

❏ How well will people be prepared? Will advance material be available and received on time?

❏ Should some people bring special information, such as reports?

❏ Is the meeting process clear? Is there time for presentations and problem solving?

❏ Are the time frames realistic? Are you taking on a six-hour issue in one hour? (If so, how far can the group realistically proceed in one hour?)

❏ What other issues or hidden agendas could hinder the effectiveness of the meeting?

Other Concerns

❏

❏

❏

5

WORKING WITH
PROBLEM-SOLVING GROUPS

Focus, Involvement, and Commitment

These are the cornerstones of the problem-solving process. They are central to everything you read in this book. Everything you and your group do must aim to strengthen these elements within the problem-solving meeting.

Focus turns ordinary light into a laser. Focus in a problem-solving meeting means staying on track, pulling together as a group, dealing with the difficult issues, and generally having all members be 100 percent there—physically and mentally. Focus makes a group powerful.

Involvement is the energy that builds ownership. Involvement generates information, ideas, and decisions; without involvement there is no group process. Participation needs to be nurtured and guided; otherwise, it won't be there when needed. It can also become misdirected, causing more problems than it solves. Not everyone knows how to participate in a problem-solving meeting.

Commitment is the result of focus and involvement. Commitment is what moves a group to become a team. Commitment does not happen on its own, but is built by paying attention to focus and involvement throughout the problem-solving meeting. Change only comes about with commitment, and change is the goal of problem solving.

When members of a group are motivated and focused, synergy is created—the group's energy is greater than that of all the individuals combined.

Problem Solving Differs With Individuals and Groups

An individual solving a problem—whether buying a car, selecting a pair of shoes, or renovating a basement—moves through each stage of the problem-solving process. As long as there is only one person involved, consensus is not a problem.

Two or more people attempting to solve a problem run into the "multi-head" syndrome—not everyone sees the issue the same way or wants to solve the problem in the same manner. If a group cannot agree on the analysis and problem definition, how can they agree on a solution? People enter a group with different life experiences and values; they see the issue from different perspectives.

One role of the facilitator is to ensure that people share their different perspectives and that everyone listens to this information.

How to Make Decisions in Groups

Build Consensus From the Outset

A group must achieve consensus on the facts and the definition of the problem. If it cannot agree on the facts, it won't be able to agree on the problem. Problem solving without consensus wastes precious talent and energy.

Take Consensus Before Compromise

Compromise means a settlement in which each side gives up some genuine needs in order to arrive at an agreement. Since people have lost something important, implementation of compromise decisions is often slow, and dissatisfaction with the decision can emerge later. With consensus, on the other hand, a person willingly gives up an old position for a new and better one and experiences a sense of gain, not loss. Decisions based on consensus, although longer and harder in the making, have a high degree of support and survival.

Manage Time Carefully

Time is the critical issue. Majority vote and arbitrary decisions can be fast, but they rarely foster the level of commitment that accompanies a consensus decision. Occasionally time runs out before the group can reach a decision. Tension increases and the process is rushed, resulting in poorly evaluated ideas and carelessly arranged action plans. If time runs out, a group can always fall back on a majority vote or an arbitrary decision made by senior management. It is best to discuss this early. Ask the group to consider their method of decision making if consensus has not been reached when the allotted time is up.

Keep Voting as an Option

Majority vote decisions leave winners and losers. But if the group agrees in advance that majority vote will be an acceptable way of deciding, then such a decision results in strong ownership by the group. With a clear understanding up front, consensus building still survives.

Use Experts

Occasionally the group does not have the expertise to sort out the facts and make a decision. Seeking an expert's advice and basing a decision on that person's recommendation can bring a sense of being let off the hook. In the end, though, members must still decide by consensus that the proposed solution is the one they wish to follow.

Avoid Rubber-stamping

A dangerous situation arises when the senior manager has already made a decision but still brings the group together. To give the illusion of group involvement, he asks for ideas toward a solution. Most people see through the guise, and frustration and anger will be the least of that manager's problems. A lose/lose outcome is certain. To avoid it, give the manager some options.

Try These Suggestions

- If the decision is final, present it as such. Perhaps a memo is more effective than a meeting. Encourage the manager to make a clear autocratic decision.
- If the manager has a strong preference but has not reached the final decision, say so and then invite opinions. Ensure that everyone knows the manager is the final decision maker. This sets the stage for group consultation followed by an autocratic decision.
- With the decision already made, but its implementation unresolved, the manager can ask the group to work out the how, rather than the what, of solution finding. Consensus can still occur.

Eight Myths About Problem-Solving Groups

Myth 1. Groups Are Not as Effective as Individuals

Many people believe that group efforts are cumbersome and a waste of time. The saying "a camel is a horse designed by a committee" reflects this attitude. Can we blame people for being cynical about meetings? How many times have you sat through boring meetings, wondering why you were there and wishing someone would take charge of the mess?

We believe that groups are ineffective when there is a lack of focus and involvement—when there are no clear roles for managing the content and process. In focused groups, by contrast, the quality of the decision usually surpasses that made by an individual.

Myth 2. Consensus Is Impossible

Consensus takes time, but it *is* achievable. Some fast shooters are unwilling to devote the time required to find "win/win" solutions. All too often, team leaders lack the facilitation skills to help a group build consensus.

Consensus decisions are marked by quality and acceptance. People who participated in the consensus decision tend to support it down the line. Consensus on final decisions must be built by a series of consensus decisions throughout the problem-solving process: from defining the problem to outlining the facts to delineating possible solutions. Consensus at each point leads to final commitment.

Myth 3. Managers Must "Give In"

Not so! Consensus means that the manager must be part of the decision—otherwise there is no consensus. Consensus is defined as "unanimity, solidarity of opinion." In reality, it describes a situation where people initially have differing views and, after discussion, change their minds and support the decision of the group.

Myth 4. Group Problem Solving Is Time Efficient

People often enter a problem-solving meeting with the notion that problem solving is quick and simple. An "over the top and home for lunch" mentality creates unrealistic expectations. To be effective, problem solving in groups takes time. Most people underestimate, by 50 percent, the time it takes to effectively solve a problem in a group.

Myth 5. Problem Solving at Work Differs From That at Home

Yes and no. The process remains the same; only the content issues vary. The major difference is the attitude and objectivity one brings to the task. At work we tend to interact in a more objective manner and use proven methods. We try to act "professionally." At home we are likely to be more vulnerable and have greater expectations of emotional support.

Myth 6. Problem Solvers Are Supercreative

Being creative can mean different things for different people. Problem solving draws on a number of talents. Initially, it requires analytical skills to dig out the facts and label the feelings surrounding the issue. Later, it benefits from playful idea generating and detailed evaluation of these ideas. Finally, problem solving demands careful planning for action.

Most of us are capable of operating in all these areas, but we have our preferences. We must be careful not to fall in love with our interests and lose patience with others' ideas. Group creativity comes from utilizing everyone's talents and preferences and being open to new perspectives. A group setting provides us with the opportunity to see issues differently and to develop our own creativity.

Myth 7. Results Are Improved If Everybody Comes Prepared

By all means, encourage people to be prepared with information about the issue. But when they bring *ideas*, they may already have defined the problem as well—possibly without the benefit of other perspectives. Coming up with a good idea naturally builds ownership. If group members arrive with a commitment to their own solutions the stage is set for conflict, and little unified group progress will occur.

Myth 8. Problem Solving Is All Left-Brained

It would be nice if problem solving were a linear process with special appeal to those with a dominant left brain (those who prefer to operate with their logical side). Some people are disappointed to discover that problem solving is much more than fixed steps from start to finish and a guaranteed outcome. Problem solving is both science and art, especially when done in groups. It is an activity that involves both sides of the brain.

Open the Door to the Right Brain

On the surface, most meetings are dominated by left-brained activities: words, numbers, sequence, order, and logic. All the while, our right brains scream for sustenance—a picture, some color, emotions—anything but black and white data. Here are a few suggestions to tap both hemispheres of the brain.

Encourage people to write. Give them a word or a statement and ask them to write down what pops into their minds. They can do this alone or in small groups. Encourage them to write freely and to silence their inner critic for the time being. Tell them that it is impossible to be critical and creative at the same time.

Take a break. When the group appears to be stuck for ideas, introduce an informal break. Instead of heading for the coffee corner, ask members to do something completely different. Suggest a brisk walk around the building; a physical exercise to relax eyes, necks, and backs; or viewing a stimulating video featuring a motivational speaker, a comedian, or an interview with someone creative.

Let information incubate. Let people sleep on data and ideas. Place suggestions in their heads overnight or between meetings; give them mental homework. You might even ask them to search for creative ideas in the books listed in the Resources section of this book.

SECTION TWO

SIXTY FACILITATION TOOLS

Introduction to the Tools

You are now familiar with the theoretical model and the skills required to bring it to life. The remaining pages describe sixty specific tools you can use to guide your group through the problem-solving process.

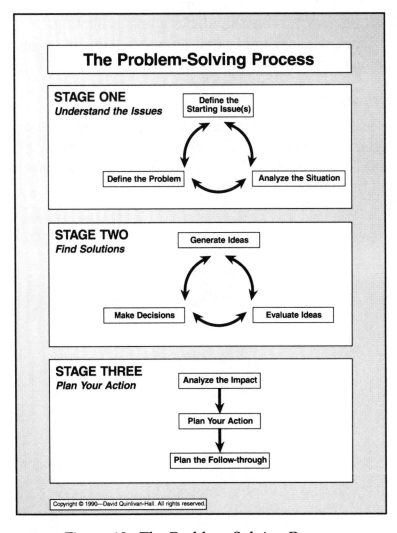

Figure 12. The Problem-Solving Process

Each of the three stages is broken into three phases. We introduce each stage with a statement of the *Objective,* followed by *Suggestions to the Facilitator* for working in this phase. Some tools are distinct interventions, others are variations on a previous tool. A small shift can be all that is required to refocus the group in a more appropriate direction; look for these subtleties when facilitating.

Once you have used a tool, be sure to write down your comments in the *Your Notes* section.

Authors' Note

We really want to hear from you. If you have suggestions arising from your use of the tools and you think they should be included in the next edition of this book, please send them to us, care of the publisher.

6

STAGE ONE:
UNDERSTAND THE ISSUES

The Importance of Stage One

Most of us are solution oriented; we enjoy playing with ideas but shun the hard work of analysis. Ask anyone around you for solutions to the nation's economic woes or foreign relations issues and he or she will have an answer. Most of us admire people who can make quick decisions; those who analyze and ponder the issues rarely get our attention.

People tend to avoid Stage One because it can be the hardest part of problem solving. It hurts to admit that there is a problem and that we are a part of it. It hurts to dig into the problem and uncover the reasons for it. Instead, we are encouraged—with demands like "give me your solutions, not your problems"—to do the opposite. If we follow that route, issues will remain buried rather than resolved.

Because Stage One can be so uncomfortable, most people are anxious to move on. You will frequently find yourself fighting against this current. "Let's move on and solve this problem!" is the battle cry.

With a clear plan and useful tools at your side, you'll find it easier to resist even your own temptation to rush ahead without thorough analysis. Stand your ground and guide the group through this important stage.

Objective of Stage One

The objective of Stage One is to define the problem and build a base of information about it. We suggest you spend 50 percent of your meeting time in this analysis stage.

Phase One: Define the Starting Issue

Objective of Phase One

The objective of this phase is to acknowledge that there is a problem. In counseling support groups such as Alcoholics Anonymous, "treatment" begins when the participant admits to the problem. Similarly, in problem solving, members must agree on the common issue and declare their willingness to work on it. They must also decide if the problem is worth solving.

Suggestions to the Facilitator

Maintain Structure

The group is looking to you for direction on how to proceed. At this early point in the problem-solving meeting, it is best to err on the side of structure and direction.

Ensure Full Participation

It sets the tone for the rest of the meeting. It enables you to discover whether the people present are the right ones to be working on the particular problem at hand. For people not interested in the problem, the meeting may be a waste of time. Question their presence; their lack of involvement can become a nuisance later. Deal with this early, before it becomes difficult and disruptive. Encourage people to leave if they can make better use of their time elsewhere. Consider asking them to be available later should the group require their expertise on a particular subject. This allows them to make a contribution without having to sit through the entire meeting.

Occasionally people are told to attend a meeting against their choice. Help these people figure out the reason for their required attendance. Offer them choices, but always remain clear that choosing to remain in the group means a full commitment to working on the problem.

Make Sure the Right People Are There

If some members are missing, it might be appropriate to adjourn the meeting until they arrive. Otherwise, the group will have to spend time backtracking.

Why Are You in This Meeting?

In one of Dave's workshops a woman said she had no idea why she was there. While she was polite about not wanting to disturb the session, it became obvious that she had "checked out." Dave suggested she call her manager during the break and find out why she had been sent. Shortly after, she announced to the group that her job was changing and that group facilitation was to be a key part of her new duties. With this new information, her participation improved dramatically.

Restrain the Group

They often want to "get into it" but are not ready yet. This is why you need to be directive. Assure them that by building a strong foundation now, the later stages will progress more quickly and thoroughly. There will be individuals who will fight you, but you need to assert yourself as the facilitator.

Keep a Good Pace

As people begin to talk about the problem, there is a temptation to say everything in the first breath, especially if the issue is a big one. Keep people focused on the topic and when the question is answered, move on.

Surface a range of opinions. It is still too early for consensus. This is the time to explore the issue from all sides and gather as many different perceptions as possible. Later the group can focus on agreement.

The Blind Men and the Elephant

Four men who were blind since birth were asked to describe an elephant. Each was led in turn to the elephant so he might touch it. The first blind man grasped the elephant by the leg and exclaimed, "So solid and stable, like a great tree; it must be a very strong, slow-moving beast."

The second man seized the elephant's trunk and remarked, "Like a large boa constrictor, supple and strong; it must be flexible and fluid when it moves."

The third man felt the elephant's tail and said, "Sleek and slender; it must be a quick, graceful creature."

The last blind man touched the elephant's ear and pronounced, "Thin, wispy, and pliable; it must be a delicate creature; perhaps it could fly."

Now who was right and who was wrong? They all had pieces to the puzzle, but none had the complete picture. Similarly, when groups meet to solve problems, individuals hold pieces of the problem, each looking at it differently. No one is wrong; everyone just experiences the problem differently.

The Tools of Phase One

The tools in this phase are all *questions*. They are your most effective tools as the group settles in and you take charge of the facilitation. Questions help members vent their feelings and explore their perceptions of the problem.

Keep questions simple; limit each to one thought. Two simple and clear questions are better than one complicated one.

Prepare the Group

To follow the suggestions in this book will mean a departure from the way most people expect to solve problems. We strongly recommend that you explain the process to the group before you begin. Show the problem-solving model and explain the newsprint posted for the group memory. Spend a few minutes defining the roles of facilitator, recorder, and group members. This is also a good time to develop a contract (see Chapter 3).

Select the Tools That Suit

We would like you to see the tools as a collection from which to draw as the need arises. One tool will work with one group, yet yield little success with another. Two tools in conjunction may work better in one setting, while a selection of two different ones will do the job another time. Your best preparation is to read through the tools one at a time so that you are familiar with them. Then, when you are planning for your next problem-solving meeting, or when you are in the midst of a session and need a helping hand, you know where to look to find the tool that might do the trick. If it doesn't work to your satisfaction, try another. There is space at the end of each tool to record your observations and experience with it.

▮1▮ *What Is the Starting Issue?*

This is an obvious question and a good place to start. It is so obvious, simple, and clear that it never fails to generate discussion.

Sometimes there is immediate agreement on the issue, but more often we find that there is more than one starting issue. Let them all come out; later the group can decide if these are variations of the same problem or distinct issues that need to be tackled separately. Now is not the time to dissect them.

Recording the possibilities is what is required at this point. Some people will want to elaborate on each issue now. Let them know that the purpose of this early exploration is to define the problem. In order to do that, a full list of issues is needed. Once a list of the starting issues is posted, you can move on.

Your Notes

2   *What Is Your Understanding of the Task?*

If you are working with a task force or committee, use this question instead of Tool 1.

This question helps groups clarify their mandate. It can elicit such responses as "We're here to come up with ideas, not to solve the problem," or "Our job is to recommend possible solutions, not to solve the problem."

Your Notes

3 *What Will Success Look Like?*

This has become our standard opening and it never fails to yield good data. The group can go in two directions here. One is to look at success in the meeting itself and interpret the question to mean: "What will success look like in this meeting?" The other direction addresses implementation back home: "What will success look like when the problem is resolved?" Typically, most people respond to the second version. Since both are valuable, either redirect when people respond, or state both questions separately. If someone says, "I want to see us work better as a team," then team member openness and communication appear to be part of the problem. If another says, "I'd like to leave with a clear idea on our personnel requirements for the Fox Lake project," then staffing and workloads are probably issues for them. As people talk, the diversity of perception emerges. In some meetings it is like dealing with oranges, apples, and papayas; in other situations everyone talks about oranges from the beginning.

The definition of meeting success coupled with the answers to Tool 1 provide the parameters for the meeting. The group's task is to close the gap between these two points, between what seems to exist now and what is desired for the future.

Your Notes

4 *Is Everyone Committed?*

The success of your problem-solving meeting depends on members being fully committed to seeking solutions. If they aren't, it is important to discover this early and deal with it.

Sometimes there are problems within problems, surface and underlying issues, or "content and process" concerns. For example, if the issue is vacation scheduling, and one member is unwilling to work on it, then the issue before the group becomes that of individual commitment, not vacation scheduling.

Interpersonal issues can be disruptive. You probably recognize the situation where everyone feels tension, but nobody wants to name it openly. That's where facilitators earn their keep. Your job is to first recognize this is happening and then pick the right moment to label it as such. Be direct; you will save time and avoid frustration. You also strengthen your credibility!

Ask your group for a clear sign of commitment when you use this tool. A verbal yes or a nonverbal head nod with eye contact confirms each member's commitment. This person-by-person check takes only a minute, but it is absolutely critical. This is the first moment of consensus building.

Try also Tool 26.

Your Notes

5 *How Do You Feel About the Issue?*

People are more likely to work on an issue they have strong feelings about. Conversely, commitment will be low if the issue has either little meaning or is poorly defined.

You can help members to focus on their feelings with any of the following interventions:

- Assess whether the group membership is appropriate. If the majority of responses are lukewarm, then you may all be wasting your time being there. Find an issue that motivates the group or adjourn.

- Balance the intensities of the emotions. An overzealous member can be as much of a problem as the person who doesn't care: one needs to be toned down; the other has to be confronted and asked to choose.

- Access the emotions of the group and individuals. Emotional data are difficult to generate, because it's not always easy to articulate emotions clearly. However, emotions increase the risk and the reward. What may have been neutral and bland can become colorful, exciting, urgent, distressing, or maddening. Release of frustration around an issue and excitement over an idea fuel motivation.

Feelings are part of the information base that the group needs to function effectively. A question like "How do you feel about the problem?" lends itself to a round-robin approach (asking everyone in the group to speak in turn). It is a good way of involving the members early. The quiet person will try to pass and not say anything. Don't push; wait or come back to them later.

You must control the degree of emotional intensity but not the emotions themselves. We caution you and the group: stay away from "playing therapist."

Your Notes

6   *Whose Problem Is It?*

It is important to be clear on who owns the problem. You, the facilitator, must never take ownership. It belongs to the group! It is important to unearth varying levels of ownership; some members have more than others. At times, the owner of the problem is not even in the room, and it may be inappropriate for the group to deal with it. Either include that person or halt the discussion on the issue.

Your Notes

7   *Are You the Right People to Work on This?*

The right participants must be present for this problem-solving process to work. For example, if a decision is required, then the key decision makers must be in the group. If the meeting touches on personnel matters, then the human resources department must be involved. If the plant workers are affected, their input is needed. If fund raising is the concern, then the fund-raising committee must be represented.

Caution: Avoid hangers-on, people who just like attending meetings. Use experts as they are needed. Limit group membership to those who have a stake in the outcome and have declared their willingness to work toward a satisfactory solution.

    Try also Tool 12.

Your Notes

8   *What is the Best, Worst, Most Likely Scenario?*

This is three questions that are often used together.

First Question

Invite the group to imagine a future devoid of the problem, then ask the following questions:

- What would be happening or not happening?
- What would the people be doing or not doing?
- How would you spend the time and money saved by not having to deal with this problem?

This usually leads to a clearer problem definition. Once the group has created a picture of an ideal world, it can contrast that vision with the present condition to discover what is wrong.

Second Question

Suppose you don't solve this problem. What is the worst thing that could happen as a result of your inaction?

Encourage members to paint the gloomiest scenario they can. Keep asking, "What if...?" People might try to duck their own discomfort by talking about others, but bring them back to how not solving this problem might affect them. Make sure speakers begin with "I" to signify ownership of what is being said. For example, "I think this...," "I feel this...," "I want this...."

Focus the group with questions such as

- How will this problem affect you?
- How will this issue affect your chances for promotion?
- How will it affect your family's lifestyle?

Third Question

Suppose you do solve the problem. What is *most likely* going to happen?

With the *best* and *worst* possible scenarios the group has painted a picture of the extremes. Now lead them to look at the more moderate middle. An exploration of the "most likely" will probably lead to answers to the questions:

- Is it realistic or feasible to proceed?
- Is there energy to work on this issue?

Your Notes

9   *How Big Is the Problem?*

Some problems are the hub of interrelated issues. The tentacles of these problems reach out and touch many aspects of the organization, the team, or the individual. Other problems merely pass as momentary blips on the landscape.

By answering this question, the group begins to define the scope of the issue. They can then decide how much energy the problem should consume—energy in the sense of time, money, and personal commitments.

If the problem is a big issue, it might be best dealt with by chopping it up into smaller chunks. By dividing the issue, the group may discover that one item needs resolution before they can proceed on others.

Discovering a sense of direction is a major step in successful problem solving and the essence of Stage One.

Try also Tool 14.

Your Notes

10 *Is It Worth Solving?*

If the group has not yet addressed this question, it is time for you to raise it. Here are a couple of variations:

- What's in it for you to solve this problem?
- Do you really want to spend all day on this issue?

By exploring the benefits of solving the problem, individuals may see why and how they can become involved. On the other hand, if the problem does not seem to be worth solving, the group might decide to move on to another area or end the meeting.

Here are a few options you may wish to put before the group. Members have the following choices:

- Ignore the problem: hope that it will go away.
- Enjoy it: see it as a challenge and find creative ways to live with it.
- Remove it: spend time and energy as a group to deal with it.
- Pass the buck: say "It's not our problem."
- Remove themselves: admit that they don't want to deal with it or that the problem is too big for them and they will let someone else handle it.

Your Notes

Phase Two: Analyze the Situation

Objective of Phase Two

The objective of this phase is to gather the facts. Investigation is the key word, and Sherlock Holmes is the model. Help the group turn the problem upside down and look at it from all sides. Attention to detail is essential.

Suggestions to the Facilitator

Take a Leading Role

It is still early in the problem-solving process and the group will be seeking direction. Structure helps.

Ensure Consensus on the Data

It is from the data that the problem definition is built; it is from the definition that the solutions are generated and the final decision is made. It is this decision that prompts an action plan and eventually changes the problem situation. Groups without commitment tend not to act. Consensus builds commitment.

If there is disagreement surrounding a piece of information and this disagreement cannot be resolved, it is better to leave the data out of the group memory than to continue the process using contentious data. It can be compared to using poor quality wood in the construction of a house; in many places it might pass unnoticed, but in the foundation it will result in future problems.

Look for Assumptions

Generally avoid them.

Place All Solutions on Hold

As the analysis progresses, solutions begin to emerge. It is important that the group does not pursue these and launch into Stage Two. However, these potential solutions do give a forward vision and this encourages the group.

Place these ideas on a sheet of flipchart paper entitled "Ideas" and post them far from the ongoing group memory, preferably out of sight. Or have group members write their ideas on notepads for later use.

11 Sherlock's Basic Repertoire

Who, what, when, where, why, and how—these are the keys to unlocking information in any situation. The possibilities and variations of these six questions are many. Here are just a few examples.

Who

"Who" questions help identify the major players in the situation.

- Who is causing the problem?
- Who is being affected?
- Who says this is a problem?
- Who has done something about the problem?

What

"What" questions seek data.

- What is going wrong?
- What are the symptoms?
- What are the consequences to others?
- What is causing the damage?
- What unusual conditions surround the occurrence of the problem?

When

"When" can be the time on the clock or calendar or a point in a sequence of events.

- When is the problem occurring?
- When was the first time this occurred?

Where

"Where" can be a specific place or a point in a sequence of events.

- Where is the problem occurring?
- Where is the problem most concentrated or felt most strongly?

Why

"Why" questions always seek the underlying cause; by asking at least five "whys," you increase the likelihood of finding the root cause and not settling on symptoms.

- Why are the work orders backed up?
- Why did only three people show up for the meeting?
- Why did donations dry up?

How

"How" questions usually relate to a process or sequence of events. We suggest you play down "how" questions because they are less focused than the Five Ws. Still, some may be useful.

- How should the process be working?
- How did the fire start?
- How are the other branches dealing with this?

Try also Tool 13.

Your Notes

12 *Are You Deciding or Recommending?*

Somewhere during Stage One the group must clarify its mandate. (If you have already done this with Tool 7, this step is not necessary.)

Determine whether group members are delegates or representatives. Delegates have the authority to make decisions. Representatives must report back to their constituents for the final decision.

Each group is different, and within groups there are often both delegates and representatives. Confusion between the roles frequently arises with volunteer organizations, such as charities and appointed boards.

Now is the time to clarify these roles. Representatives may need extra time to report back to their departments and receive instructions for decision making. In some cases, representatives may be replaced by delegates or be given authority to make decisions.

Try also Tool 7.

Your Notes

13 Is/Is Not

Exploring what is working well can be as fruitful as looking at what isn't. Knowing where the problem is *not* occurring allows the group to narrow its search and ultimately uncover where the problem is taking place.

"Is/Is Not" ensures that both positive and negative sides to the situation are included in the data. Here are some questions to help you dig out information.

- Who is involved?
- Who is not involved?
- Who is affected by the problem?
- Who is not affected by the problem?
- When is it occurring?
- When is it not occurring?
- Where are the symptoms being experienced?
- Where are the symptoms not being experienced?
- What aspects of the process work well?
- What aspects do not work well?

Caution: When a group begins to look at what is working well, it must remain in the past or present. Data from areas working well today and yesterday are useful and factual. The trap springs open when a group begins to speculate about tomorrow, thinking about what *might* work well. Now they shift from analyzing the situation to generating ideas (from Stage One to Stage Two). It's still too early for that.

Try also Tool 11.

Your Notes

14 *Break Down the Problem*

With this tool you can help the group to break the issue into understandable and manageable pieces. Vague problem statements tend to overwhelm us by their magnitude. Here are some examples.

- The company is going belly up.
- Our relationship is a mess.
- Deliveries are too slow.
- The volunteers don't know what they are doing.

While such broad statements are natural starting positions, they are of little value for problem solving. By their magnitude, they discourage participation, promote generalization, and invite procrastination.

Help the group to dissect the issue. This enables them to understand the issue better and moves them toward solving it. Success with the first few bites encourages people to continue with the next.

Your Notes

15 *Separate Facts From Assumptions*

Assumptions have a way of getting mixed in with facts. Removing them is an ongoing process. Listen for assumptions; they don't have the same solid tone as facts do and often the person putting an assumption forward will sound tenuous. If you suspect an assumption, ask the group or the individual, "Is this a fact or an assumption?"

Periodic reviews for assumptions help to keep the data pure: ask, "Is everything here a fact or have we allowed some assumptions to creep into the data?" The same question can fill the void when there is a lull in the process.

Your Notes

16 *Force-Field Analysis (I)*

This technique can be used to analyze a problem situation. The group identifies pressures or forces that either strongly support a situation or strongly resist it. The term *force* here refers to the influences that impact upon a set of circumstances. It helps your group sort them according to their positive and negative nature, thus clarifying an overwhelming mass of data.

Follow a five-step procedure.

1. State the issue clearly. Examples: What prevents this organization from attracting new talent? What keeps us from being the best in our field?
2. List all factors that may influence the situation.
3. Identify the listed items as either driving or restraining forces.
4. Arrange the two lists on separate sheets of paper and number each item for reference.
5. Discuss the items and their relative impact.

This is as far as you let the group go in the analysis phase. Later on, during solution finding, force-field analysis can be applied to make decisions about the various forces.

See also Tool 49.

Example

David recently worked with a committee that had expressed concern about its effectiveness. As Step 1, he asked them: "On a scale of 0 to 100, how do you rate your current effectiveness as a team?" After some discussion and simple arithmetic, they settled on a score of 66. For Step 2, Dave recorded their specific examples of factors they saw as contributing to the rating. In Step 3, they listed first the forces "making you 66 percent effective," then those "that prevent you from reaching 100 percent." From there, they quickly moved through the remaining steps, with reminders to avoid premature problem solving.

Your Notes

17   *Ask an Expert (I)*

Be clear that the expert is not being asked to make the decision. At this stage the group is gathering data and a good expert is another source of valuable data.

When to Call an Expert

In a session for a small business owner and his associates, the starting issue was "How do we move the company from sole ownership to a corporation with shareholders?" As the meeting progressed, it became obvious that the group did not have the expertise to proceed further. They decided that someone who knew about financial and legal options was needed. Dave asked the group to list the competencies required of such a person. They developed an action plan to find the expert and one group member agreed to make the necessary arrangements. The meeting was adjourned and met again with the expert present.

Tips on Using Experts

- In advance of the meeting with the expert, ask the group to prepare a list of the key issues for which the expertise is required.
- Give the list to the expert for advance preparation.
- Start the meeting with your agenda and obtain agreement from the expert to cover these items first. This is a contract between the group and the expert. You then stay with the group's structure and maintain control of the process. Should the expert try to control the group or attempt to make the decisions, you must step in, politely but firmly.
- Ask the expert to attend only part of the meeting, just long enough to provide the information the group needs to move ahead on its own. Explain this

to everyone in advance and when the time comes, thank the expert, call a break, and reconvene without the outside helper.

Your Notes

18 *Review the Group Memory*

A review of the group memory is a way of taking stock of what has been going on. In the thick of problem solving, something might be missed; a review gives everyone time to stop and see what has been happening. It quickly shows where the group has to go next.

When participation slows down, a review can be a beneficial filler to spark new thought. Periodic reviews of the memory give the group a measure of accomplishment.

This review, in the midst of the process, should be about five minutes long. The facilitator quickly touches on the key points and gauges the mood of the group. Too much detail and a slow pace will bore rather than uplift the group.

A review after a major break (lunch, overnight, a week) must be more detailed and takes more time. The level of detail is proportional to the length of time a group has been away from the data. Therefore, a review after lunch might be five minutes; a review first thing in the morning seven minutes; and a review after a week's absence might take ten to fifteen minutes. As a rule, do not take longer than fifteen minutes.

See also The Group Memory in Chapter 3.

Your Notes

Phase Three: Define the Problem

Objective of Phase Three

The objective of this phase is to find the "real" problem. As the group moved through Phases One and Two, understanding of the starting issues expanded, and the issues themselves changed. Occasionally the change is minor; sometimes an entirely new issue comes to light—the "real" problem everyone has been looking for. Knowing the real problem can be as exhilarating as solving it.

Suggestions to the Facilitator

Look for the "Aha" Experience

You can see it in their eyes when the lights go on. There will be yelps of surprise and sighs of relief when the "real" problem has been found. It may come to some sooner than to others, so make sure everyone catches on.

Don't Move on Unless the Problem Is Defined

The temptation is strong to move prematurely into Stage Two, particularly if it has been a lengthy analysis phase. Resist going ahead without a clearly defined problem that everyone can support.

Watch for Problems Within Problems

If the wheel of a car is bent, it must be fixed before the tire can be balanced. Search for the root cause beneath the surface symptoms.

19 Define the "Real" Problem

It is useful to keep reminding the group that the immediate goal is to clearly define the problem. Defining the problem three or four times is not uncommon.

After a period of information gathering, pop the question, "What, in your estimation, is the 'real' problem?" and then proceed to redefine the problem. With each new definition, the problem becomes clearer.

The recorder should keep a separate sheet of paper entitled "the real problem is..."; this will focus any subsequent deliberations the group may have.

Defining the Problem

Two hikers are being chased by a grizzly bear. While on the run, one of the hikers reaches into his backpack and pulls out a pair of jogging shoes. The other hiker glances over and says, "Why bother? This bear can outrun you even with those on." His partner responds with, "I don't need to outrun the bear, I just need to outrun you."

Your Notes

20 *State the Problem As a Question*

Problem definition works well if it ends with a question mark—a question invites an answer. "To develop a plan to obtain new marketing funds" is not as effective as "What do we have to do to get this new program funded?" "How can we sell more books?" yields more ideas than "Developing a marketing plan to increase book sales."

If you need to prime the pump, use any of the following to get the creative juices flowing.

- "How" suggests a process.
- "Where" directs us to locations.
- "Who" identifies the people involved.
- "When" points to time.
- "What" sorts out process and content.

Your Notes

21 Define the Key Terms

This tool ensures that everyone is talking about the same thing. As you listen to the comments in the room, do you sense that people interpret certain key words differently? If a clarification is needed, use this quick intervention.

1. Find the problem definition on the group memory. If it is buried among other data, ask the recorder to post it on a separate sheet.
2. Highlight the components of the statement.
3. Ensure the group agrees on a common definition for each.

Agreeing on a Definition

Peter sensed that members had diverse interpretations of the task. He suggested they take a moment to discuss and agree on the key terms of their problem definition. It read:

How to (develop) a |fund-raising project| for the (summer.)

Peter highlighted the key words and then facilitated the discussion of their meaning. Here are some points the group raised.

|fund-raising project|

What will it be? Are we talking about a cookbook, a nature guide, a raffle, a series of Sunday events, a concert? What amounts do we hope/need to raise? Who will be involved in raising the funds? What group are we targeting with this fund-raising drive?

When exactly does this have to be in place? By the start of the tourist season? How much time do we have between then and now?

Are we here to come up with ideas or specific plans? Who will do the work?

In the end, they agreed on a much clearer definition. To decide whether to publish a cookbook that

a. Appeals to a national audience

b. Can be ready by June 1

c. Can be done with no more than $2,000 start-up money

d. Could raise at least $5,000 over two years

Your Notes

22 *Picture the Problem*

Ask the members to close their eyes and picture the problem in their mind's eye. Most of us are visually oriented—all we need is to be encouraged to apply that talent. Ask the group to describe their images or draw them on flipchart paper.

Pictures are not restricted to architectural or engineering issues. People who work with computers can picture software, marketing people their customers, personnel people their staffing dilemma, and volunteer organizers their goals.

Many people, when asked to draw a picture, become self-conscious about their lack of artistic talent. Tell them it's all right to draw stick figures and other simple forms. If someone is really reluctant to draw pictures, ask them to "picture" the issue in words using headings and different colors to chart the issue.

See also "Left Brain/Right Brain" in Chapter 1.

Your Notes

23 Compare Starting Issue With the "Real" Problem

A comparison of the starting issue and the newly defined problem raises a number of possibilities.

- The "real" problem is the same, but more clearly defined.
- The problem has changed, becoming a much larger issue, with the old problem contained within it.
- There is a totally new issue.

If the issue is new, ask what happened to the old one. Determine whether a new issue has been adequately analyzed. If it has not, embarking on a new round of analysis may be met with resistance. The group has struggled to this point and may be exhausted. Expecting to succeed, they discover a new issue in need of further analysis. What should you do?

Instead of tackling more content, move to a feeling level. This gives the group a needed break, yet still involves analysis. Ask questions about the feelings of the group, such as the following:

- How do you feel with what you have discovered about this issue?
- What do you want to do now?
- Is this a good time for a break or to adjourn for the day?
- Are you ready to forge ahead?

In this way you reward the group for work already accomplished and point out the benefits of identifying the "real" issues. Your goal is to help the group work through any disappointment so that the group members can enjoy their accomplishments.

If there are now two or more issues, you must ask the group to order them in some fashion: by importance, by complexity in random order, or using any sorting procedure that makes sense.

Your Notes

24 *Build a Problem Definition*

At times the definition is not obvious, yet everyone in the group has a piece of it. The purpose of this tool is to collect these perspectives and build a complete definition.

Ask people to write their definition of the problem, beginning with "What" and ending with a question mark. Putting these definitions on flipchart paper helps focus the group.

Now look for the common elements and distill them down to one statement. Once this is formed, return to those items not included in the definition (the uncommon elements) to see if they should be included or rejected. The person who initially proposed the point should have the final say on whether it stays or goes.

This is an opportunity to employ the "straw man" intervention with three variations:

- You can include your own definition of the problem with those of the group.

- Between sessions, you and the recorder compile possible definitions and present them to the group. Your suggestions may provide the catalyst for further ideas from the group.

- A subgroup of two to three members adjourns to build possible definitions and then presents them. Ideally, the subgroup should work during a regular break, so that the group is not waiting and losing energy.

See also "Straw Man" in Chapter 3.

Your Notes

25 *Separate the Issues*

Occasionally there are three or four separate, but related, issues. Trying to lump them together just does not seem to work. Keeping them distinct makes them easier to define and eventually solve.

Once a number of issues are defined, the group can set priorities through these questions.

- What is most pressing?
- Is the resolution of one problem dependent on or affected by the resolution of another problem?
- Which issue will bring the best return of group investment?
- Are we the right people to be working on all these issues?
- Which issue are we most motivated to tackle first?

See also the example in Tool 21, where a discussion of one problem definition yielded several subissues.

Your Notes

26 *Check on Commitment*

With Tool 4 you determined the varying levels of commitment of group members. But as the group progresses, this commitment will undergo change. For some, the initial commitment was shaky, and now that the going is getting tough, their resolve is weakening. Others, initially strong in their commitment, discover that this process takes more work than they bargained for. As a result, the group needs to reassess its commitment. Long, drawn-out meetings, stretching over hours or, in the case of committees, over weeks and months, further add to the danger of erosion.

Do not assume that the levels of commitment remain unchanged, just because you obtained a nod from everyone during the first hour. Check it out! If it's fading or gone, explore why and determine what it takes to bring it back. One thing is certain: the group cannot go on without it.

Try also Tool 4.

Your Notes

27 What's Already There?

It is hard to know where to place this tool because it can fit easily into either Stage One or Stage Two. It is placed here because it is primarily a data-gathering question. Yet when people think about "what already exists" or "what has been tried before," there is an immediate connection to solutions, something your group is not ready to address. This tool makes a good transition from Stage One to Stage Two, and that is why it is the last tool in this section.

This is a flexible tool. It can assist in triggering ideas and generating data. Looking at what already exists may identify an "off-the-shelf" solution with a direct fit or one requiring only slight modifications. Not having to redesign and build from scratch is cost-effective in terms of time and money. Most people and organizations like to use what they already have.

A Case in Point

Dave worked with an in-house task force to generate ideas for improving internal communications. When someone suggested a newsletter, all but two members ridiculed the proposal. This idea had been tried before and had bombed. Although Dave played the role of devil's advocate against the newsletter, the two who supported the idea convinced and motivated the others to give it another try. They showed how the company and the circumstances had changed. They also suggested specific approaches to overcome past shortcomings. An old, failed idea became part of a new consensus decision.

Your Notes

The Key to Stage One: A Review

One of the great myths about problem solving is that the most important part of the process is coming up with ideas. Too many people believe this and, as a result, are ineffective problem solvers. Many creative idea generators are poor problem solvers.

The effective problem solver spends 50 percent of the time defining and analyzing the issue. Understanding the problem requires patience and determination. Such hard mental work deserves recognition—give yourself (and your group) a pat on the back for a clear definition of the problem.

If unsuccessful dieters spent as much time researching and understanding their weight problem as they spend trying out new solutions, they might discover the "real" problem—and perhaps a solution that would work for them!

Once more, for emphasis, if the group has uncovered the real problem and completed a thorough analysis, the time has come to enter Stage Two.

7

STAGE TWO: FIND SOLUTIONS

W elcome to Stage Two. Up to now, you probably felt as if you were holding back on the reins of a runaway horse. Stage Two is a release from that tension. Now the group begins to speculate on the future rather than being restrained to look at the troublesome past. With your help it can now apply the full force of its creative ability to actually solve the problem.

Objective of Stage Two

The objective of this stage is to achieve a consensus decision on the best possible solution(s).

Phase One: Generate Ideas

Objective of Phase One

The objective of this phase is to generate ideas that may lead to possible solutions.

Often groups have difficulty thinking beyond what they already know. They need your guidance to expand their solution horizons and think creatively. Generating ideas is a lot like playing, and many of us have forgotten how to play.

Few issues have just one right answer; the solution is usually found in a range of possibilities. The challenge for your group is to find the solution that best fits the environment in which it will have to survive. Policies, funding, timing, staffing, and ethics are some examples of these environmental conditions.

Suggestions to the Facilitator

Encourage the Group to Play

Make this phase lively and energetic. Help people return to their creative, childlike selves. Some will resist, since playing has become synonymous with not working. Having fun is essential now—and it is legitimate work!

Involve Everyone

Let members participate in their own ways and in a manner that makes them feel comfortable.

Stay Out of the Way

Let the group take off and "free-think" in all directions. You and the recorder must ensure that everything is captured in the group memory. Keep track of time.

Bring Back Solutions Put Aside Earlier

Many potential solutions have already surfaced and may sit among the notes on the walls.

28 *Brainstorm*

It seems everyone has brainstormed at least once, yet few actually know the rules. The rules give the technique its structure; without them much is lost.

Rules for Brainstorming

1. State the target clearly. For example, ask, "How can we double the number of volunteers?" or "How can we handle the XYZ project without increased staffing?"

2. Set the group size. Five to eight people is ideal for this purpose; if there are more in your meeting, form two groups with the same instructions or with separate topics.

3. Give the following instructions:

   Strive for quantity. Ask members to come up with as many ideas as they possibly can.

   No criticism is allowed. Tell the group that there are no impossible ideas at this stage and the crazier their proposals the better.

   Build on the ideas of others. Ask them to flip ideas over, propose the opposite, add to them, and piggyback on others' ideas.

   Talk in headlines. Short and snappy responses are preferred.

4. Constantly encourage and reward the group.

5. If the group bogs down, have people review the group memory to think of opposites, variations, add-ons, etc. Make this quick and lively.

6. To facilitate the flow, use two recorders if contributions come faster than they can be written up. Halfway through, switch recorders to alter the makeup of the group.

Brainstorm With Bach

When the mind and body are relaxed, retention and recall is enhanced. Certain music relaxes us and tends to stimulate right-brain thinking. Play it softly in the background during brainstorming. Record stores carry collections with titles like "Relax With the Classics." The music has a perceptible tempo between 50 and 70 beats per minute and is designed to diffuse and release energy trapped in the body. Handel, Telemann, Vivaldi, and Albinoni are some of the composers; look for their largo, adagio, andante, and pastorale movements.

Your Notes

29 *Ask an Expert (II)*

Sometimes, when a technically complex solution is called for, or there is a narrow range of possible solutions, the group needs an outsider's expertise.

Give the expert a clear definition of the problem, the data collected, and the evaluation criteria. Use the expert to help a group generate options, but maintain control of decision making.

In the end, true to their commitment to decision by consensus, it is the group, not the expert, who must decide.

See also Tool 17.

Your Notes

30 *Theories and Concepts*

Often, part of a group's action plan consists of reviewing relevant literature. You might provide the group with a relevant article or book. A reading assignment between sessions helps to educate members for the evaluation of the many ideas they have generated. As a variation, ask for one or two volunteers to read and report their findings at the next session.

Such an infusion of new ideas is especially useful with groups caught in negative ruts, signaled by such cries as "We've tried that before" or "Nothing will make a difference around here."

Try also Tool 27.

Your Notes

31 Pass Along Your Ideas

Here members can make their contribution without having to compete for air time. If you want to know what they are thinking about a given topic, ask each to write a response on a piece of paper and then pass it to a neighbor. That person adds another point and passes the paper along. Each addition can be new or a variation on points already recorded. Let this run for a few minutes. Restrict the topic and replies so that recording and subsequent processing can be handled quickly.

Use a Variation

If your group is large and you want to save some time, ask small groups to work on a sheet together, then pass it to the next group and receive the other group's sheet in turn. Use flipchart paper and colored pens and give groups plenty of room to work. Ask for contributions in headline form.

Instead of Rotating the Sheets, Rotate the Groups

This can be a refreshing break without interrupting work. Ask people to gather around two posted sheets, give them space between groups, tell them to select their own recorder, and off they go.

Watch the Time

We find that contributions come quicker, and usually are of higher quality, if members operate under some pressure. Too much time leads to digressions and a loss of focus. Keep the pressure up, make demands for work, and balance such activities with frequent short breaks and large-group activities.

Review the Data

Review the generated data with the full group. Bring all sheets to a central location and ask members to get off their seats to come and look at what they have collected. Consensus is not required for this idea-generating activity.

Avoid Cliques

If you frequently utilize small-group activities, you may find that subgroups form around viewpoints and social affiliations. Counteract this trend by mixing up individual and group tasks. *Always* come back to the full group for review.

Change Seats

After breaks and prior to the next activity, invite members to change where they are sitting in the room. Tell them, "You'll be amazed how your point of view is affected by where you sit in relation to others and the group memory."

Your Notes

32 *Construct a Matrix (I)*

Matrix listing is a good technique to access the logical thinking talents in the group. To explain how it works, let's look at what Dave recently did with a group of managers in a strategic planning session.

The company had five functional departments: A. Operations, B. Engineering, C. Marketing, D. Administration, and E. Sales and Distribution. The plan for the future included four points.

1. Improve customer service.

2. Encourage entrepreneurial thinking.

3. Finance growth primarily from internal resources.

4. Establish a research and development group.

The problem had been defined as: "What can we do to achieve our vision?" Dave suggested the use of a matrix to get the group to explore the dynamics between departments and vision statements. First, they developed a simple grid.

VISION	DEPARTMENTS				
	A.	B.	C.	D.	E.
1. Customer Service					
2. Entrepreneural					
3. Growth					
4. R & D					

Figure 13. Matrix

Then they looked at connections and possibilities. Dave primed the pump with questions like these.

- What can Operations do to build a stronger customer base?
- Should it be done for the company at large or strictly within the department?
- Can Engineering become more entrepreneurial?
- What can Marketing contribute to R&D?

Your Notes

33 *Post It*

This tool energizes and provides visual relief. It is based on the storyboard technique developed by Walt Disney.

The method is simple. People write their ideas on large index cards or self-stick removable notes, one idea per card. If someone wants to elaborate on an idea or give an example, it can go on the bottom or back of the card. The ideas are then posted to the group memory. Ideas can also be in the form of pictures and photographs.

The memory might already include major categories around which people generate ideas and under which they place their cards. At other times it can be a wide-open brainstorm.

This tool has some interesting pros and cons. On the plus side is the opportunity for all members to create ideas at once without loss of information or a slowdown in the process. Rearranging ideas is easy, since each idea has its own card. Categories help to focus ideas and reduce future sorting time.

The drawback is that some people get caught up in their own ideas and can't hear or read those of others. You can remedy this by reading ideas aloud before posting. This tool does not work well if there are more than six people because the cards may be too small to read from a distance. If this is the case, you may decide to use larger cards or break into smaller groups.

Your Notes

34 Guided Fantasy

On a guided fantasy, you ask people to imagine some place, some event, some circumstance. In problem-solving meetings, it can be used to imagine a world where the problem has been solved.

A Day in the Future

We suggest a three-step approach to using a guided fantasy.

1. Set the scene and explain the process.
2. Conduct the guided fantasy. Speak slowly. If possible, play relaxing music and dim the lights.
3. Debrief (what did you experience?) and generalize (how does this relate to your present situation?).

Peter used a guided fantasy with a career-planning group. They had aired their frustrations at the many obstacles to change. He proposed a guided fantasy as a way to tap the right-brain hemisphere.

With relaxation music (described in Tool 28) playing in the background, he explained, "I am going to ask you to imagine a day five years in the future. Somewhere in your subconscious mind there are some pictures of how you'd like the future to be. Let's go and look there, each of you in your own way. Let's go daydreaming." He then asked participants to relax, "Please sit comfortably, close your eyes, inhale deeply and exhale slowly, three times."

Next, he conducted the guided fantasy. "As you pay attention to your own breathing, shut out any distractions from this room. Continue to breathe slowly in and out. Now imagine yourself waking up, on a workday, five years from now. Go slowly. Imagine your eyes opening and take in what you see. What time is it? Are you alone? If not, who is with you? Do you wake up to an alarm clock? Do you have to get up right away? As you take in the room, look out the window. What do you see there? Just before you get out of bed, look ahead in your day. How will you start? How will you dress? What's for breakfast? Who else is there with you? Do you stay at home or do you go elsewhere to work? What kind of work do you do?"

All questions were given slowly and quietly, with thirty to sixty seconds in between. After about ten minutes, he gently ended the guided fantasy. "I am going to ask you now to leave that day in the future and come back to this room."

Finally, Peter began the debriefing. "Before you speak to anyone, please write down what you saw and heard in the fantasy. Write it down like a diary. Later on we will look at what you might want to do to move your current activities toward achieving what appears to be your wish for the future."

The example suggests how guided fantasy can be inserted to change the pace and to unearth some interesting data. Some people will complain that they were unable to follow; put them at ease by saying that this works better for some than for others. They'll probably enjoy hearing others' stories.

Your Notes

Phase Two: Evaluate Ideas

Objective of Phase Two

The objective of this phase is to sort through the ideas generated in Phase One and find those that have the best chance of solving the problem.

The time has come to test them against the harsh reality of the world "out there." The group must now establish criteria against which to evaluate their ideas.

First, take a break between generating the ideas and evaluating them. Even five minutes can help people put their feet back on the ground and their minds back into reality. Prepare them before the break by saying, "Take five minutes to stretch and come back with your knives sharpened. Be prepared to cut up, throw out, and move around what we have here."

Then pose these questions to help the group set criteria for evaluation.

- How practical is the idea?
- Is it realistic?
- Is it cost-effective?
- Can it be easily implemented or does it require extensive convincing of others?
- Is the idea consistent with the directions already being undertaken by the company?

Suggestions to the Facilitator

Check Your Time

Choose one of the following evaluation tools based on the quantity of proposals the group has created. If the group has fifty items from a brainstorming session, it could take hours to review each individually.

Prevent Quick Assessment

If the problem solvers are allowed to jump to quick decisions about the solutions based on their personal criteria, then battle lines will be drawn and egos put on the line. It then becomes difficult to have them think in new directions and consensus takes longer.

The key to this phase is to establish the common criteria before allowing any individual judgment.

35 *Accentuate the Positive*

This technique invites people to think positively before launching into criticism. It adds an upbeat energy and keeps the focus on the ultimate purpose of all this hard work.

Ask members to state three things they like about the idea being discussed. Smiles and nods of approval emerge when people are being positive. New ideas spin from positive thinking, as people notice the value of the idea and continue problem solving around the concerns.

This also works well when there are personality clashes in the group. By stating the positive, the sniping person often ends up focusing more on the idea than the person.

Your Notes

36 *Pros and Cons*

This is quick and easy and works well when evaluating a small number of ideas. Take one sheet of flipchart paper per idea being evaluated.

Figure 14. Pros and Cons

Different headings yield different explorations. Use the same process as above; we suggest you stay away from the words "good" and "bad"; they are too value laden.

Your Notes

37 *Must Have*

This technique helps the group sort the ideal from the practical. Suppose a group has made long lists of ideas of how a staffing situation might be solved. These ideas, however creative, must now be evaluated in the light of reality. "We can do almost anything, except hire new people": this is nonnegotiable; any solution must not involve hiring more staff.

Ask your group to come with its own must-have list. Some of these constraints will be dictated by outside circumstances; others will be established by the group. With this list in hand, each of the possible solutions can be judged. It either fits, or it doesn't!

Examples of Evaluation Criteria

- Must be consistent with hiring policies and practices.
- Must have a good chance to be accepted by senior managers.
- Must not add to our operational budget.
- Must fit into our existing workload.
- Must achieve the results by year-end.
- Must not harm the environment.
- Must use the existing office space.
- Must include all members of the team.

Your Notes

38 *Internal and External Constraints*

All problems and solutions exist within a world of constraints—usually time, money, and people. Other constraints come from the organizational culture, politics, environmental impact, the competition, etc. Defining constraints addresses the question: *"Who or what do we have to watch out for that could block the solution of our problem?"*

When you ask your group to determine the constraints acting upon their work, you move them from the broad to the specific; broad data usually trigger specific examples. See the following example.

Internal Constraints

- What constraints might each department place on the solutions? List data by department.
- What constraints might certain groups in the organization place on a solution (for example, management or the union)?

External Constraints

- What groups outside the organization will be affected by the solutions (for example, customers or local government)?
- What constraints might these groups place on the solutions?

The Impact Analysis in Chapter 8 draws on the outcome of this activity and will provide a good check of how thorough you were here.

Your Notes

39 *Leave It to the Expert*

Experts can be of great help when developing criteria. They know the field better than most and can often quickly identify the critical issues. They can also point out the finer points that the group might overlook. Often it is the small things that will frustrate implementation.

Please refer to the points in Tool 17 to get the best help from the expert while ensuring that the group makes the decisions.

How Credible Is the Expert?

Before turning to an expert, ensure that everyone agrees that the individual is the right choice. One person's expert might not be acceptable to someone else. The criteria for using an expert should be sorted out before the group invests the time.

See also Tool 17.

Your Notes

40 Construct a Matrix (II)

The process here is the same as in Tool 32. The criteria are listed across the top and the ideas down one side. This enables the group to match each idea with each evaluation criterion. It is easy and thorough. The number of items is limited by the size of paper and wall space available.

Evaluation Matrix

The problem definition reads: "How can we improve communications throughout the office?" The evaluation criteria are that the solution:

A. Must be within existing budget constraints.

B. Cannot add extra staff.

C. Must be easy to implement.

D. Must not pose problems to customers.

E. Must have long-term impact.

IDEAS	EVALUATION CRITERIA				
	A.	B.	C.	D.	E.
1. Remove Partitions		✓			
2. Floor Plan A.		✓			✓
3. Floor Plan B.	✓	✓		✓	✓
4. More Greenery (Plants)	✓	✓	✓	✓	✓
5. More Windows		✓		✓	✓
6. Music		✓			
7. New Furniture		✓		✓	✓
8. Move		✓			✓
9. More Parties/Lunches	✓	✓			

Figure 15. Evaluation Matrix

Using the matrix, it appears that solutions 3 and 4 are the first choices of this group.
     See also Tool 32.

Your Notes

41 *Sorting*

With the mass of data and the many possible solutions stored in the group memory, you need to offer the group a method of sorting information. There are a variety of sorting methods; use whichever suits the needs of your situation.

Duplication and Connections

Quickly go through the ideas, looking for duplicates or similar thoughts that can be combined or deleted.

Rank Ordering

This helps to sift a large number of ideas down to a workable few. Ask each person to select the top three choices of the ideas presented. From this list the group can proceed with a more critical evaluation using such tools as 32, 36, 37, and 40.

Categories

Placing ideas in suitable categories helps focus the group. For example, try using departments, divisions, line and staff groups, and needs internal and external to the organization.

Candidates for Deletion

On any list of ideas there is at least one item that can immediately be removed. Get rid of it early and maybe others will follow (but watch that the group doesn't get carried away). The rule of thumb is that if it is a quick unanimous decision, it goes; if there is any doubt or dissension, the idea stays for a more critical review. Protect a few of those fringe and off-the-wall thoughts, but not against the strong wishes of the group.

Your Notes

Phase Three: Make Decisions

Objective of Phase Three

The objective of this phase is to select a solution or a number of solutions that the group feels will resolve the issue(s).

The problem-solving process has been building to this point, and this is an exciting period. However, members may resist this point for fear of making a wrong decision. There are always some who feel that not deciding is better than making a wrong decision.

Suggestions to the Facilitator

Gently Nudge the Group

Do this especially if there is reluctance due to fear of making a wrong decision. If it stems from new evaluation data, then return to Phase Two and immediately clear up the issue. If you do not, consensus will be affected.

Allow Evaluation to Flow Into Decision

The boundary between evaluation and decision making is invisible. Evaluation is the distillation of ideas until a decision is made, thus decision making is the end of the evaluation process and not actually a separate phase.

Expect Disappointment When the Decision Is Obvious

Some decisions may appear anticlimactic and are reached without fireworks going off.

Highlight, Circle, or Star the Decision

Make a bit of a fuss about it, especially if there is a sense of disappointment. Give the group a break, arrange for a round of refreshments, offer cookies with the coffee—think of a surprising way to reward them for working so hard.

Keep the Group on Track

The process is not over. There is still work to be done. Remind the group to return for the important step of action planning.

Clarify Whether the Group Is Making Decisions or Recommendations

If there is any doubt, and it has not been clarified earlier (Tool 12), now is the time to do so. Delegates normally are empowered to decide; representatives cannot make decisions unless they first check with their constituents.

42 The Nominal Group Technique

This one comes in handy when time is running out and the group has more than four solutions to consider. It is a form of majority voting and should be used only when a decision is essential and time does not permit further discussion. This technique can only be brought into play if the group has agreed to a majority vote as their fallback decision-making option. If voting is not part of the group contract, then the contract should be reviewed and agreement should be obtained to use this process.

Although it is a form of majority vote, you are not abandoning decision making by consensus! To explain, let's assume that the group is facing six possible solutions. Proceed as follows:

1. Ask each member to look over the list of solutions and assign to each a rating from 6 to 1, with 6 denoting the solution that *best* meets the criteria and 1 the solution that *least* meets it. It is important that participants continue to use the evaluation criteria to make their decisions and not revert back to personal preference. Do not ask them to vote, but to assign priorities in view of the evaluation criteria.

2. Collect the ratings from each member; add them up or have the recorder do so. The highest score has the greatest support; the other solutions fall into priority order according to score.

3. Check the level of consensus. Will all support the decision 100 percent, even though it was made by a form of voting? Often support is high, especially since everyone is aware of the time pressure and a genuine attempt was made to achieve consensus.

4. If there is no consensus, ask the dissenters what bothers them about the decision. Ask what needs to be changed, added, or deleted.

Your Notes

43 *Add and Delete*

Consensus at this stage can be difficult. Something may be missing from or too much included in the final decision. Focus the group on adding or deleting the necessary pieces. Here are a few sample statements to explain what we mean.

- To *add:* "Sarah, are we correct in saying that you want to see a major review of office locations as a part of this decision?"

- To *delete:* "Devon, this piece about the citizens' committee seems to be bugging you. Group, how can we maintain the thrust of this solution and still deal with Devon's concern?"

Ensure a smooth-fitting solution and increase the chances for a smooth implementation.

Your Notes

44 Have It All

Many times a group ends up liking all the solutions that have been generated. If you are in doubt about the feasibility of implementing all the decisions, play devil's advocate: throw roadblocks at the group. If they are committed to the solutions, they'll fight hard now and will also fight hard when it comes to implementation.

There is occasion later, during impact analysis in Stage Three, to test the feasibility of using all solutions.

Your Notes

45   *Check the Pulse*

There will be times when you need to know which side of the fence people are sitting on. We have used two quick interventions.

Take a Vote

You are not making a decision, only testing the water. Keep it informal: "I have a sense we are getting to the end of this discussion. By a show of hands, how many of you want to go on for a while?" Or say, "This may be important. Put up your hand if this issue should be included." With the count of votes as data, the group can decide which way to proceed.

Speedy Memo

This is another way to find out what people are thinking— without a lengthy discussion. Use it when you aren't sure what the mood is or where people are heading. Ask everyone to take a small piece of paper and reply with a word or short phrase. When the energy seems to be low, ask: "How do you feel right now?" When people appear to be going in several directions at once, ask: "How can we get back on track?" The advantage of the speedy memo is that contributions are made anonymously and even the most reluctant participant will respond. Collect the papers and quickly read them aloud. No names are mentioned. The outcome usually gives new direction to the group's deliberations. It also saves you from having to label the unspoken.

Your Notes

46　Overcome Blocks to Consensus

If consensus has broken down along the way—and this will happen—the group has the option of *agreeing to disagree*, using majority vote, or passing the decision to someone else. If, however, consensus has been maintained to this point and only now begins to break down, we offer a few suggestions to bring it back on track.

Be Soft on People and Hard on Issues

What is preventing the dissenting individual(s) from accepting the group decision? It is time to be specific and focus on each person who is disagreeing. Do it in a gentle but firm manner. The group must hear why this person finds it difficult to accept the position of the majority. Perhaps it's not the entire decision that poses a problem, only part of it; sometimes a slight change of wording can bring a person on board. Many things can stand in the way of consensus, but these blocks can only be addressed if they are out in the open.

Turn to the Group

Once the information has surfaced, turn the issue over to the group. The group has to find ways to support and bring the person into the consensus, not to criticize the individual for ruining it. At times, you need to be a buffer between the person and the group, letting both sides know that effective problem solving means everyone being open and honest. Let the group know that conflict is natural, and that it can be sorted out.

Use Peer Pressure

This is the opposite of the above. Here the group is permitted to pressure the person holding out. Occasionally people are stuck, and a little pressure helps. This may be the appropriate tool for the job, but be careful not to alienate anyone.

Talk About Something Else

Changing topics relieves the pressure and gives the person time to think. Upon returning to the topic the person might have had a change of mind. Even taking a refreshment break or moving flipchart paper can help things cool off.

Refer Back to the Group Contract

You might say to the group, "You agreed earlier that if a consensus decision was not achieved, all your work would go over to the board to make the decision. Is this what you want now—or is there a way through this block?" You can now increase the pressure by adding, "You have come this far with consensus, it would be a shame not to get a decision by consensus." If a little guilt will loosen the logjam, use it.

Contract for Decision Making

If there is no initial contract, then now is the time to establish the decision-making options. Review the position and present the options. For example, "You are stuck and there doesn't appear to be much chance of clearing this up in the time remaining. You have just a few options available. You can vote, pass the decision to the board, or agree to come back for yet another meeting. Can anyone see another option...? What do you wish to do?"

Your Notes

47 *The Last Point of Agreement*

If the group begins to lose focus and break into factions, turn to the group memory and find the last point of agreement. Do not let people become entrenched and take sides now.

Take them back to the evidence of last consensus to remind them how far they have come and how hard they have worked to get to this point. Praise their past wins and rekindle their belief that it can happen again.

Your Notes

48 *Clashing Values*

Not everyone shares the same viewpoints on how the world should work. Value clashes are one of the most trying situations to deal with in a problem-solving meeting.

When all reason and logic has found its way to the group memory and the parties still choose to disagree, *there is a values clash*. At this point you can proceed in one of two directions: agree to disagree and attempt to move through the value differences to a common ground or move to a values clarification strategy.

Naturally, the first option is the easiest as long as value differences don't cause a major disruption. If they do, then the only alternative is to deal with the clash head-on. You might start off by saying, "What can we do in the next fifteen minutes to resolve this issue and get back on our original track?" Give the issue back to the group and begin problem solving.

Don't spend more than thirty minutes on a values clash between two people—it's a waste of the group's patience. If the issue cannot be resolved to a workable point, more time won't make much difference. (We are assuming that during this time all members are involved in sorting out the issue; otherwise, even five minutes spent on a two-person issue is a waste.) You may wish to ask the two to meet after the sessions to work things out or give the group a break and help the two to come to some understanding.

Your Notes

8

STAGE THREE: PLAN YOUR ACTION

Once a solution has been selected you may find it difficult to keep the group in the room. Members often feel that the work is finished and want to leave.

But a lot of questions still need to be answered: Who is going to implement the solution? What needs to be done to ensure success? Can this decision stand on its own in the real world? What will be the impact on the folks next door? What are the likely roadblocks to this new direction? Who needs to be informed, by when, and by whom?

Objective of Stage Three

The objective of this stage is to "reality test" the group's decision and to build a workable action plan.

Once the idealistic thinking has been knocked out of the decision, does it still hold up? If the answer is yes, then action planning follows.

Items overlooked throughout the problem-solving process tend to turn up in Stage Three, and at times the group must return to an earlier phase to deal with these. A new issue can surface and it might require further analysis. This can frustrate the group, especially if they think they are done.

As always, the final decision rests with the group, but cutting corners in Stage Three is like attaching cheap speakers to top-of-the-line stereo equipment. Thousands of dollars invested in amplifiers, tape decks, and compact disc players are wasted if the sound is delivered by poor-quality speakers. Similarly, all the hours and energy spent in Stages One and Two can be lost if Stage Three is not completed with care.

Stage Three is more linear than the preceding stages. The impact of a decision must be explored before moving to an action plan; without it, solutions can cause more problems than they solve. While in Stages One and Two there was frequent back and forth movement; Stage Three flows in sequence, with one phase following the next.

Phase One: Analyze the Impact

Objective of Phase One

The objective here is to decide whether the group is ready to proceed with implementation.

Impact Analysis deals with the positive and the negative effect of a decision on people and systems. The group now looks at the stumbling blocks as well as the supports for the decision, at the obstacles and the opportunities.

Suggestions to the Facilitator

Seek Balance

"Blue sky" thinking is over. Who are the levelheaded thinkers in the group? Look to them for balance.

Factors That Might Block or Support Implementation

Hurdles to implementation are easily perceived, but their opposites are less obvious. Seek out examples of supporting factors from the group's own circumstance. For example, "The fact that the budget will be cut by year-end creates a good climate for your proposal," or "Based on what customers are telling you, the time seems ripe for a program like this."

Push Hard for an Honest Assessment

It is better for a poor decision to die in the meeting than to let it flop in public. Going back to Stage Two means extra work now, but will be far less of a headache than going ahead with a half-baked decision.

Look Back at the Evaluation Criteria

They usually contain good impact assessment data.

Create Excitement

After turning the decision upside down and pulling it inside out during impact analysis, the group will feel eager to go out and implement it. Keep that excitement alive!

49 *Force-Field Analysis (II)*

You saw this technique earlier (Tool 16), as part of the situation analysis phase. Now, during the action planning, you can use it with an extra step. In it, the group grapples with the question of how to alter the impact of the forces.

Using force-field analysis at this stage, the group identifies the forces that either strongly support a situation or strongly resist it. Members then sort these forces according to their positive and negative nature and decide on ways to modify their impact.

Follow a Six-Step Procedure

1. State the issue clearly. Example: "What may prevent the implementation of this solution?"

2. List all factors that may have an influence.

3. Sort the listed items into driving or restraining forces.

4. Post the items on separate sheets; number the items for reference.

5. Discuss the items and their relative impact.

6. Explore how driving forces can be strengthened and restraining forces weakened.

See also Tool 16.

Your Notes

50 *Blocks and Supports*

This is an elaborate version of Tool 49 (Force-Field Analysis). It pushes the group to explore in detail the helping and hindering elements they perceive.

Blocks to Implementation

Examine possible blocks: "Is there anything out there that will *kill* our plans before we even get them up and running?" "What's likely to *delay* the implementation?" Look at the Five Ws.

- *Who* is likely to get in the way, both inside and outside the organization? Examples of inside interference might include other departments, interest groups, or key decision makers. Outside interference could come from customers or clients, governments at various levels, competitors, neighbors, or suppliers.

- *Why* would they not support you?

- *What* are they likely to do to stop you or slow you down? *What* policies or procedures might hinder implementation?

- *When* might the blocks appear?

- *Where* will they take place?

Supports to Implementation

This is the flip side of blocks. Ask the group what type of support already exists.

- *Who* is going to be on your side both *inside* and *outside* the organization?

- *What* is already out there that will support your decision? Think of trends, decisions already in place, accepted practices that link with the ones being proposed.

- *When* is the best time to gather support?
- *Where* is support the strongest?
- *Why* might support be forthcoming?

See also Tool 49.

Your Notes

51   *What Could Happen When...?*

The previous tools focused on what might happen prior to implementation. With this one, the group speculates about the results of change in the system. While this is speculation, most people know their own organization and what is likely to work and not work. If they don't, they shouldn't be trying to change it.

Here are a few questions to define the nature of the impact.

- What groups or individuals will be most affected by the implementation of this decision, inside and outside the organization?
- How will they be affected?
- Who will be least affected, inside and outside the organization? Why?
- What will be the short-term impact? Define short term; it might mean two weeks or six months.
- What will be the long-term impact? Define long term; is it a month, a year, five years, a decade?

Your Notes

Phase Two: Plan Your Action

Objectives of Phase Two

The objective here is to delineate a clear implementation plan. The group will decide what, when, where, and how this will happen; who is going to bring it about; and how they will measure success.

You need to ask the group: "Are you prepared to take action?" If a clear commitment is forthcoming, proceed. If there are hesitations, you must confront the group and clear up the obstacles.

Suggestions to the Facilitator

Cover the Bases

Use the familiar who, what, when, where, and how.

Push for a Specific Action Plan

See that the group works through it systematically and quickly. Groups are often on their last ounces of energy by this time.

Use Timelining Methods

This is especially needed for complex projects. See your librarian for details on such methods as Critical Path, Performance Evaluation Review Technique (P.E.R.T.), and Gantt Charts.

52 *How to Implement*

The group knows what it wants to do and now needs to work out the mechanics. Implementation steps must be identified before names and dates can be assigned. Sequencing these steps is another important task at this time.

An Implementation Example

A group decided to start an employee orientation program. After the members determined the key points of such a program, Dave helped them to explore the details of implementation. They agreed to take the following steps:

- Investigate what other organizations were doing.
- Review the literature in this area.
- See what resources were available at headquarters.
- Discuss cooperative efforts with other departments.
- Involve people who have had experience with similar programs.

The group assigned names and deadlines to these investigations; everyone agreed to report back in a month.

Your Notes

53 *Who, What, When?*

Volunteers are not easy to find, and even when they do come forward, the selection process continues. Be prepared for the pregnant pause as everyone waits for someone else to go first. You can move things along by subtle prompts and eye contact; once someone offers to take a task, the ball is rolling.

Keep an Eye on Group Consensus

It must remain intact through to the end! If a member offers to take on a task, the entire group should consent. In some cases, someone else in the group or elsewhere in the organization might be more suitable. Maybe it is too much for one person and two people need to take it on.

If the Wrong Person Volunteers for the Job

What happens if a "weak" member volunteers to take on a critical piece of the project? The motivation may be there, but there are doubts about ability. Your job now is to assist the group with this dilemma without causing embarrassment to anyone. Shift the focus from the person to the qualifications.

1. First, put a halt to people putting their names to tasks.

2. Next, start a list of skills and knowledge required to succeed with each task. The group develops a profile of the successful candidate for the task.

3. Match group members to the profile by asking, "Who should be taking on this part of the plan?" The decisions become obvious. We find that people tend to disqualify themselves or ask for backup in their weak areas.

Don't let success be spoiled by the wrong people taking on crucial parts in the implementation. It is the implementation that will be scrutinized by the outside world, not the long hours of deliberation. This is one of those times when your facilitation skills are seriously tested.

Establish Time Frames

When a name goes on the board, a time must go beside it. Work with each person to set realistic time frames. Pushing the time forward works better than allowing too much time. Letting things drag on too long drains the momentum. A group is energized by quick wins; the organization also likes to see immediate impact and feel that something is happening. If the time line is too loose, express your concerns. Unless there is an important reason, all action should be started within a week.

Your Notes

54 *Create a View of Time*

In addition to the sophisticated scheduling techniques mentioned earlier, here are two practical techniques that can be used without formal training.*

Looking Back

Ask each member to take a sheet of writing paper and spend about five minutes writing about the implementation of the decision. As a reference, give them a specific day in the future, a month or a year from now—whenever the implementation should have been completed. Now ask them to look back on the implementation phase and address such questions as: What happened? Who did what? Were there any surprises or disappointments? Ask members to write this as a letter to a friend or as a news release. Encourage them to include facts and feelings.

When the time has elapsed, invite people to take turns reading their story to the group. Direct the recorder to keep minutes in point form. This activity will reveal some personal information the group needs to be aware of.

An Implementation Calendar

A calendar gives the group a realistic and factual look at what lies ahead. It can be constructed in a six-step fashion.

1. Identify the steps involved in implementation.
2. Arrange the steps in chronological sequence.
3. Estimate the time needed to complete each step.
4. Determine the date by which implementation should be complete.

---

*These two techniques were adapted from *Life Work Planning*, by Arthur G. Kirn and Marie O'Donahoe Kirn. New York: McGraw-Hill, 1976.

5. Counting back from that date, assign actual dates to each step, both start and completion, to arrive at a time line. Some steps will have to be completed before others; some can be tackled concurrently. Keep an eye open for special events, such as holidays or vacation periods, that could interfere with implementation.

6. Assess how realistic the expectation is. If needed, the group can now adjust the implementation schedule by making allowance for extra time, tightening up slack periods, or revising some steps.

Your Notes

55 Tell the World

Conventional wisdom tells us to inform and involve those who will be affected by change. Most people agree, yet many forget to do it.

Alert the group to the dangers of poor communications. They now must develop a communications plan to address these questions:

- Who should be informed about the plans?
- When should we tell them?
- What concerns will people have with the proposal?
- How will we present the information?
- How much detail is appropriate?

Ask one or two members to draft all announcements from raw data for group approval. This is the group's chance to tell the world how it made the decision and how it envisions successful implementation.

For projects divided into phases, the group needs to decide on the "how" and "who" of communications at key intervals.

Your Notes

56 Until We Meet Again

The call for another meeting should be part of an action plan. If no one brings this up, then you should be sure to do it. It opens the door to Phase Three: Plan the Follow-through. Although the real work begins after implementation, the group has to think about it now. Push for a date to ensure that the problem-solving process will be completed. A firm date for follow-up stimulates people to fulfill their commitments.

Your Notes

57 *Success!*

The subject of success has already been addressed in Tool 1. Review that data on the group memory and amend it in light of the implementation plan. If something is unclear, deal with the question now. The group must decide what information about results will be useful and who should collect it.

An Action Plan Example

A group decided to start an in-house newsletter. The plan included securing approval from the owner and finding people from each department to contribute news. Only then would they go ahead with the full implementation. The group assigned specific tasks among themselves and agreed to meet in a week. Their plan was realistic and the results were measurable. They would have no problem recognizing success!

Your Notes

Phase Three: Plan the Follow-through

Objective of Phase Three

The objective of this phase is to plan a process to review the results of implementation.

During this phase, the group might encounter new issues that demand new rounds of problem solving.

The group also schedules follow-up meetings to enhance team spirit and support volunteers with the tasks they have taken on. Although follow-through usually occurs after implementation, it can start earlier. Periodic evaluations are valuable; if things go askew, the action plan can be adjusted before much damage is done.

Closure

There comes a time when the project is over. Closure is a legitimate event in the life of your group. There will be a mix of feelings, ranging from sadness to relief, from frustration to satisfaction. Aim for a finish on a positive note!

Suggestions to the Facilitator

Prepare for new rounds of problems. Action has taken place, so the situation has been affected and changed—and new data will emerge. Data are collected in the follow-up phase and may be the start of a new round of problem solving.

58 *Evaluate Results*

When a solution has been implemented, the group needs to determine how successful it has been. Individuals have different pieces of information that must be assembled to put together the whole picture for the group. Here are some data-gathering questions.

- What happened? Ask each person responsible for an item to give a report.
- Who is on board, and who is not?
- Where and when has the impact been positive and negative?
- How does the actual impact compare with what you anticipated?
- What is blocking implementation?
- Who within the group can help with this item?

This is data gathering and Stage One techniques apply. For example, with an action plan consisting of ten steps, allow two hours for the first follow-up meeting and one hour for subsequent meetings. You'll find that people become more task focused and self-disciplined with experience, and this reduces the meeting time.

If a major issue pops up, don't jump into it immediately unless it interferes with further discussion. Finish the follow-up on all items, then come back to the new items with Tool 59.

Your Notes

59 *Any New Issues?*

This goes back to Tool 19. New issues usually emerge in two forms: they are either ones that were previously discussed or they are entirely new. It could be that old issues were not sufficiently dealt with and members bring them up again out of frustration or fear they might be forgotten. Ask: "How important is this issue at this stage? Can you live with it being 'parked' for now, as you move ahead with the implementation?"

If the issue is important, old or new, the group has to decide on its next move. Ask: "Do you want to deal with this now, or are you prepared to start a fresh round of problem solving? When and how do you want to do this?"

See also Tool 19.

Your Notes

60 Congratulations and Goodbye!

Whether the meeting lasted an hour, a day, or it was stretched over several weeks, you all have worked very hard. Now is the time to celebrate the achievement. Before everybody rushes off, arrange for a brief ceremony to acknowledge the effort and exchange appreciations.

Your Notes

RESOURCES

Warm Ups

Bianchi, Susan, Jan Butler, and David Richey, *Warm Ups for Meeting Leaders*. San Diego, CA: Pfeiffer & Company, 1990.

Hart, Lois B. *Saying Hello: Getting Your Group Started*, 2nd Edition. King of Prussia, PA: Organization Design & Development, Inc., 1989.

Kirby, Andy. *A Compendium of Icebreakers, Energizers, and Introductions*. Amherst, MA: Human Resource Development Press, 1992.

Pfeiffer, J. William (ed.). *The Encyclopedia of Group Activities*. San Diego, CA: Pfeiffer & Company, 1989.

Closing

Hart, Lois B. *Saying Goodbye: Ending a Group Experience*. King of Prussia, PA: Organizational Development & Design, Inc., 1989.

Values Clarification

Simon, Sidney B., et al., *Values Clarification: A Handbook of Practical Strategies for Teachers and Students*. Hadley, MA: Values Pr., 1991.

From Left Brain/Right Brain to Creative Thinking

Buzan, Tony. *Use your Head*. London: BBC, 1989.

Buzan, Tony. *Make the Most of Your Mind*. New York: Simon & Schuster Trade, 1986.

Buzan, Tony. *Use Both Sides of Your Brain*, 3rd Edition. New York: NAL/Dutton, 1991.

Edwards, Betty. *Drawing on the Right Side of the Brain,* Revised Edition. Los Angeles: J.P. Tarcher, 1989.

Koberg , Don, and Jim Bagnall. *The Universal Traveller, a SoftSystems Guide to Creativity, Problem-Solving and the Process of Reaching Goals.* Los Altos, CA: Crisp Publications, 1991.

Nadler, Gerald, and Shozo Hibino. *Breakthrough Thinking.* Rocklin, CA: Prima Publishing, 1990.

Rico, Gabriele L. *Writing the Natural Way: Using Right-Brain Techniques to Release Your Expressive Powers.* Los Angeles: J.P. Tarcher, 1983.

Springer, Sally P., and Georg Deutsch. *Left Brain, Right Brain,* 3rd Edition. San Francisco: W.H. Freeman, 1989.

von Oech, Roger. *A Whack on the Side of the Head: How to Unlock Your Mind for Innovation.* New York: Warner Books, 1990.

Adult Education

Brookfield, Stephen. *The Skillful Teacher.* San Francisco: Jossey-Bass, 1991.

Cross, K. Patricia. *Adults as Learners.* San Francisco: Jossey-Bass, 1991.

Gagne, Robert M. *The Conditions of Learning,* 3rd Edition. New York: Holt-Reinhart-Winston, 1985.

Kolb, David. *Experiential Learning: Experience as the Source of Learning and Development.* Englewood Cliffs, NJ: Prentice-Hall, 1984.

Knowles, Malcolm. *The Adult Learners: A Neglected Species.* Houston, TX: Gulf Publishing Company, 1978.

Mager, Robert. *Goal Analysis.* Belmont, CA: Fearon, 1984.

Teaching and Facilitating

Hart, Lois B. *Faultless Facilitation: A Resource Guide for Group and Team Leaders.* Amherst, MA: Human Resources Development Press, 1991.

Renner, Peter. *The Art of Teaching Adults: How to Become an Exceptional Instructor & Facilitator.* Vancouver, BC: Training Associates, 1993.

Silverman, Mel. *Active Training: A Handbook of Techniques, Designs, Case Examples, and Tips.* San Diego, CA: Pfeiffer & Company, 1990.

Training Design

Kemp, Jerrold E. *The Instructional Design Process.* New York: HarperCollins, 1990.

Renner, Peter. *The (Quick) Instructional Planner.* Vancouver, BC: Training Associates, 1988.

Rothwell, William J. and H.C. Kazanas. *Mastering the Instructional Design Process: A Systematic Approach.* San Francisco: Jossey-Bass, 1992.

Team Building

Covey, Stephen. *The Seven Habits of Highly Effective People: Restoring the Character Ethic.* New York: Simon & Schuster, 1989.

Covey, Stephen. *Principle-Centered Leadership.* New York: Summit Books, 1991.

Doyle, Michael, and David Strauss. *How to Make Meetings Work.* New York: Jove Pubns., 1986.

Francis, Dave. *Fifty Activities for Unblocking Organizational Communication.* Brookfield, VT: Ashgate Pub. Co., 1987.

Francis, Dave, and Don Young. *Improving Work Groups: A Practical Manual for Team Building,* Revised. San Diego, CA: Pfeiffer & Company, 1992.

Harper, Ann and Bob. *Skill-Building for Self-Directed Team Members*. New York: MW Corp., 1992.

Kinlaw, Dennis C. *Team-Managed Facilitation: Critical Skills for Developing Self-Sufficient Teams*. San Diego, CA: Pfeiffer & Company, 1993.

Kinlaw, Dennis C. *Developing Superior Work Teams: Building Quality and the Competitive Edge*. Lexington, MA: Lexington Books/San Diego, CA: Pfeiffer & Company, 1991.

Johnson, David, and Frank Johnson. *Joining Together*, 3rd Edition. Englewood Cliffs, NJ: Prentice-Hall, 1987.

Miller, Lawrence, and Jennifer Howard. *Managing Quality Through Teams: A Workbook for Team Leaders & Members*. Atlanta, GA: Miller Consulting Group, 1991.

Phillips, Stephen L., and Robin L. Elledge. *The Team-Building Source Book*. San Diego, CA: Pfeiffer & Company, 1989.

Rees, Fran. *How to Lead Work Teams*. San Diego, CA: Pfeiffer & Company, 1991.

Schmuck, Richard, and Patricia Schmuck. *Group Processes in the Classroom*. Dubuque, IA: Wm. C. Brown, 1992.

Scholtes, Peter R., and contributors. *The Team Handbook: How to Use Teams to Improve Quality*. Madison, WI: Joiner Assocs., 1988.

Shaw, Marvin. *Group Dynamics: The Psychology of Small Group Behavior*. New York: McGraw-Hill, 1980.

Tagliere, Daniel. *How to Meet, Think, and Work to Consensus*. San Diego, CA: Pfeiffer & Company, 1993.

ABOUT THE AUTHORS

David Quinlivan-Hall is a hard-working facilitation trainer with degrees in education and organizational dynamics. From his family base in Nova Scotia, consulting and speaking projects take him all over North America. As senior partner of Solution Finders, Inc., he is available to provide team facilitation and change skills training. David can be reached at (902) 864-2660 by phone or (902) 864-5447 by fax.

Peter Renner spent his early years in the hotel business. After completing graduate studies in adult education and counseling psychology, he worked for twenty years as a training consultant. He now runs his publishing empire from an island in British Columbia. Peter has written two books on adult education techniques and now lives on an island off Canada's west coast. Contact him at (604) 732-4552 or fax your inquiry to (604) 738-4080.